GOLFWELL

Guidebook Vol. 1

THE SCORING EDGE:

Golf's Top Coaches on How to Hit It Farther, Think Smarter, and Score Lower

Cordie Walker

Golfwell Guidebook, Volume 1: The Scoring Edge: Golf's Top Coaches on How to Hit It Farther, Think Smarter, and Score Lower
Cordie Walker
www.golfwell.co
To report errors, please send a note to hey@golfwell.co.

Editing by Cordie Walker

Cover, Illustrations, and Book Design by Haley Anderson

Proofreading by Haley Anderson

ISBN 13: 979-8-9944910-0-3

First edition 2026. Published and printed in the United States of America by Cordie Walker in 2026.

For those obsessed with getting better.

Golf just happens to be the teacher.

TABLE OF CONTENTS

CONTRIBUTORS

(in order of appearance)

Contributor	Website	Instagram
Mark Blackburn	blackburngolf.com	blackburngolf
Scott Fawcett	decade.golf	decade_golf
Ralph Bauer	tourreadgolf.com	ralphbauergolf
Dylan Wu		dylan_wu59
Dr. Luke Benoit	rypgolf.com	dr.luke.benoit.golf
Jon Sinclair	sinclairgolf.com	jonsinclairgolf
Will Robins	thescoringmethod.com	willrobinspga
Dr. Sasho Mackenzie	thestacksystem.com	sashomackenzie
Liam Mucklow	mygolflab.ca	liammucklow
Nick Clearwater	golftec.com	nick.clearwater
Mark Crossfield	crossfieldgolf.com	crossfieldmark
Kolby Tullier	the-stable.com	kolbywayne

INTRODUCTION

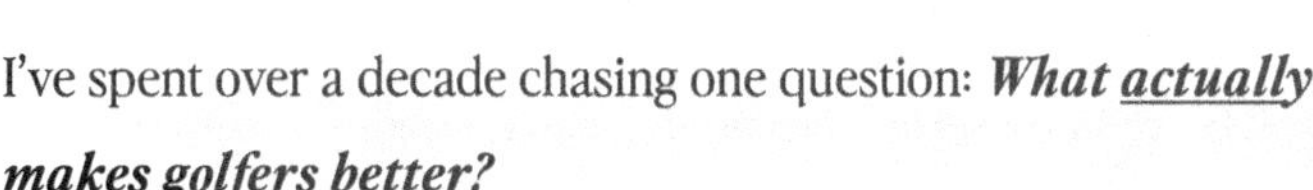

I've spent over a decade chasing one question: ***What actually makes golfers better?***

Not what "sounds good." Not what gets clicks online. What ***actually*** works when you step onto the range with limited time and want to ***actually*** get better.

I'm just like you – a normal guy obsessed with golf. I played competitive junior golf and never felt like I reached my potential. I wanted to see what top coaching was all about.

So that's what I've been doing for the past 10+ years.

That quest has taken me inside the teaching studios of the top ranked coaches in the world, onto practice ranges with tour players, and into strategy sessions with coaches who've helped tour players cut strokes through smarter decisions.

The insights were incredible – but the problem? I keep forgetting them.

The Big Problem with Trying to Learn

Here's what I noticed: After filming a video with a world-class coach, I'd be fired up. I'd take notes. Maybe even try the drill that week. But three months later? I couldn't remember that amazing idea I learned. Six months later, I'd forgotten it entirely.

I'd watch my own content and think, "Wait, when did we cover that?"

The information was scattered across years of YouTube videos, dozens of podcast episodes, and hundreds of email newsletters. I just couldn't find it when I actually needed it.

How This Guidebook Came Together

I created this first for myself. ***I needed a single reference I could actually use.***

So I went back through all the articles, podcasts, and videos from the past year of content, watched them two or three times, took some notes, and figured out the most important points you'd want to remember and the drills you'd want to try out.

Then I distilled it all down into the sections you're holding now. And we're kicking off this journey with Volume 1 of our Golfwell Guidebook series (hopefully of many more to come)!

What You're Holding

This isn't a book you read once and then put on a shelf. It's a working manual designed to live in your golf bag. Think of it like a tour player's yardage book, but instead of course notes, it has the key concepts, drills, and frameworks you need for your game.

This book is designed to be marked up. Circle the drills you want to try. Fill in the tracking sheets. Take notes in the margins when something works.

Flip to the section you need right now. Struggling with green reading? There's a formula for that. Can't make a swing change stick? There's a progression that works. Hitting terrible wedge shots? There are specific setup keys that fix it.

Come back to it before practice sessions. Reference it between rounds. The goal isn't to work on everything at once. It's to have the right info available exactly when you need it.

Start with Your Keys

On the next two pages, you'll find space for your key notes. As you work through this guidebook, certain concepts will stand out, and ideas you know you need to try.

Write those down here. These become your personal reference, the specific reminders you need. Then, before you play or practice, flip to these pages first. Give yourself the reminder you need.

The Real Reason We Do This

After more than a decade studying improvement, here's what I believe.

Golf is the vehicle. The real work is bigger. When you commit to getting better at golf, ***actually*** better, not hoping for a magic swing tip, you train focus. Patience. Discipline. The ability to stick with a process when you'd rather just hit balls.

You build humility. Improvement is slow.

You build resilience. Progress stalls.

You learn to separate signal from noise.

Golf is a game, but it's also a mirror showing how you approach difficulty, setbacks, and growth.

Let's Get Started

Grab a pencil and flip to a section that addresses something you're struggling with. Pick one drill, then do the work. ***Try it!***

Don't try to absorb everything; just find one thing that helps you improve today, then come back again and find the next one.

That's how this works. That's how you actually get better.

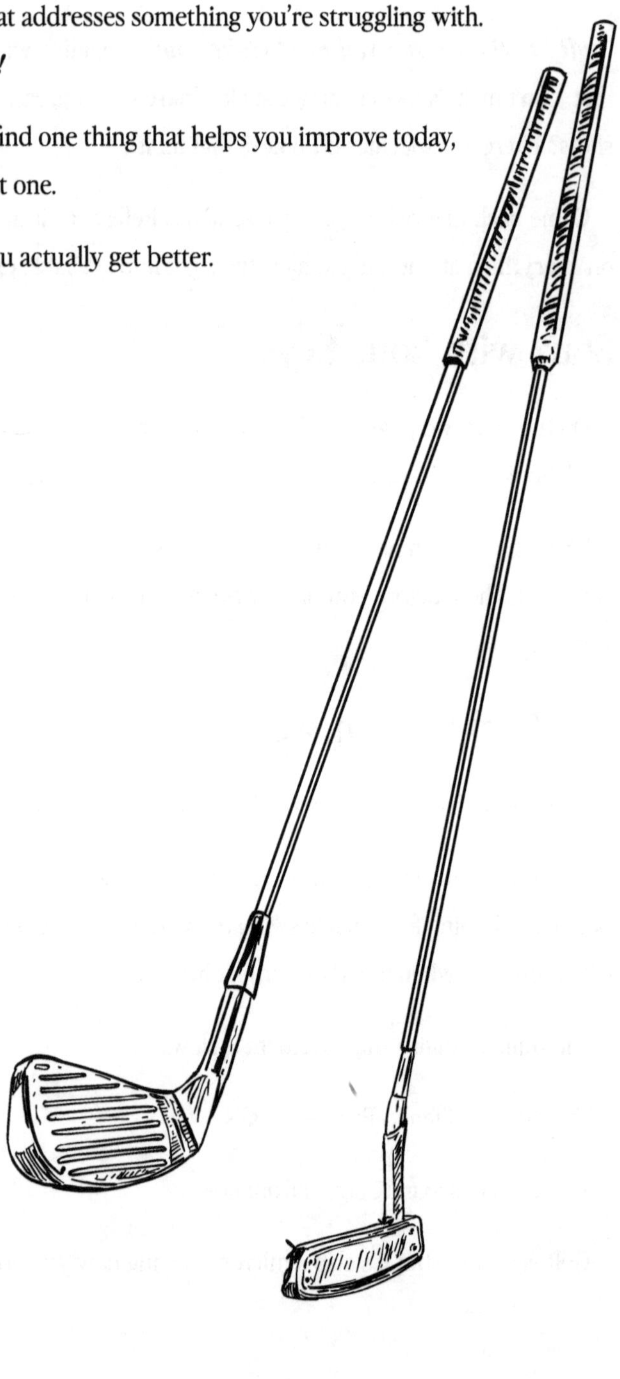

My Key Notes to Remember

For My Next Round:

For My Next Practice Session:

GUESTS OF GOLFWELL

GOLFWELL - GOLFWELL - GOLFWELL

Learn from some of the most interesting people in golf.

SIX TEACHING TACTICS THAT MAKE MARK BLACKBURN THE #1 COACH

blackburngolf.com

blackburngolf

See the full video here!

Spending two days with Mark Blackburn made it clear why he's ***Golf Digest's #1 teacher*** and works with loads of top players on tour. His coaching blends biomechanics, tech, and a deep understanding of how golfers move and think.

If you've ever tried to fix a swing flaw and you just couldn't figure out how to make the change, you're not alone! Try these ***highly effective teaching tactics*** that take into account how your body moves, how you apply force, and how you actually learn.

Tactic #1: Start with the body.

"If you don't know how someone moves, you don't know how they should swing."

A common mistake many golfers make is assuming they can fix their swing mechanics without addressing their physical limits.

A lack of mobility in the hips or restricted thoracic rotation can cause poor compensation patterns, leading to early extension or a steep downswing. Rather than forcing a golfer into an unnatural position, Mark always wants to make sure the swing is built around what the body can ***actually*** do.

Let's get started with some tests:

1. **Hip Rotation Test:** Stand on your lead leg and rotate your hips. If your range is limited, clearing your hips in the downswing may be difficult.
2. **Disassociation Test:** Hold your shoulders still and rotate your lower body. If they move together, you may struggle with proper sequencing.
3. **Glute Bridge Test:** Lie on your back with knees bent and feet flat on the ground. Lift your hips toward the ceiling while keeping your core engaged. If you feel the strain in your lower back instead of your glutes, it could indicate a weakness in your posterior chain, which can contribute to early extension and a lack of lower body stability in the golf swing.

Try This: The Foot Flare Test

1. Stand in your normal golf posture.
2. Flare your lead foot 45 degrees and retake the hip rotation test.
3. If mobility improves, try keeping your foot flared while hitting shots, and see what changes.

Tactic #2: Use the ground right.

"If you don't understand how you use the ground, you don't understand your swing." One thing Mark made crystal clear: ***if you're not using the ground right, everything else falls apart.***

With force plates, he showed how pressure shifts through the swing and ***how most golfers mess it up by mistiming vertical forces.***

Instead of pushing early in transition, they hang back, push too late, and the chain reaction begins: hips thrust toward the ball, posture collapses, and bad contact starts to happen.

Tactic #3: Use video and biofeedback for faster learning.

"Feeling is not reality. Video and biofeedback help golfers match what they feel to what is actually happening." One of the most frustrating parts of golf? Feeling like you're making a big swing change... and then seeing the video and realizing it looks exactly the same.

That disconnect between ***feel*** and ***real*** is why feedback matters so much.

Mark leans into tools like video, mirrors, and force plates to give players the kind of real-time feedback you can't ignore. It's the fastest way to close the gap between what you ***think you're doing*** and what's ***actually happening.***

Some biofeedback tools to use:

- Live Video Feedback
- Force Plates
- Mirrors
- Alignment Cues
- 3D Motion Capture

Tactic #4: Feed the fault.

"Sometimes the best way to fix a problem is to make it worse – on purpose." It sounds backwards, but it works: instead of avoiding the mistake, Mark has players exaggerate it.

Most golfers don't even realize how deep their movement patterns are ingrained. By ***feeding the fault,*** Mark forces golfers to feel just how wrong it is... and that contrast makes the right move easier to feel.

He'll literally pull you into your flaw with a resistance band so you have to fight to get into the right movement. Your body figures it out fast and the fix starts to stick.

Tactic #5: Get more adaptable with variability training.

"You don't get better by repeating the same thing perfectly. You get better by learning how to adjust." One of the biggest problems when making swing changes is that players often try to make a movement "just right" without ever gaining awareness of what "too much" or "too little" feels like. Mark's solution? ***Variability training.***

Golfers need to build adaptable swings they can self-correct and only making swings in ideal conditions that same way over and over doesn't create lasting changes.

Tactic #6: Let the body teach itself through constraint-based learning.

"If you give someone a rule, they'll spend all their time trying to follow it. If you give them a task, their body will figure out how to solve it. That's a much better way to learn movement."

TRY THIS: THE GOLDILOCKS EFFECT

1. **Underdone:** Do the movement with too little exaggeration.
2. **Overdone:** Exaggerate it way too much.
3. **Just Right:** Find the balance between the two.

"The brain learns movement through contrast. If you only ever try to do it *'just right,'* you won't know how far is too far or not far enough."

Telling someone to "stay in posture" during a shot usually isn't going to fix early extension. Rather than instructing golfers to eliminate bad habits, Mark will build constraint-based drills that naturally create the correct movement.

It works because ***your brain learns best by solving problems in real time,*** not by trying to remember another tip mid-swing.

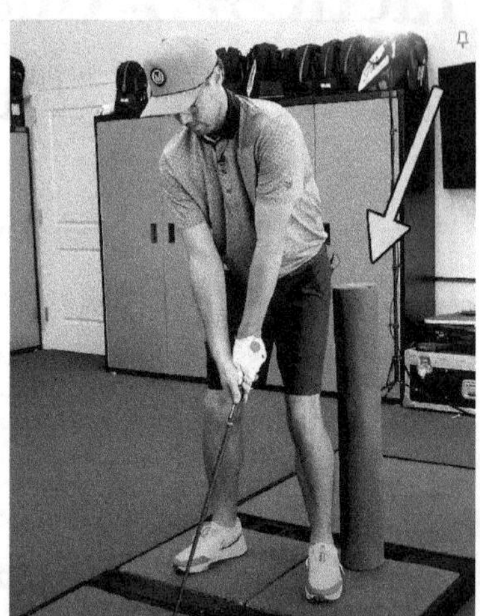

Drills to try:

- **Foam Roller:** Place a foam roller behind your lead hip to make sure you hit it during the swing (see right).
- **Obstacle-Based Drills:** Use alignment sticks or barriers to guide movement without overthinking.
- **Pressure-Based Feedback:** Mark might physically hold a golfer's shoulders still to train body disassociation.

DRILLS TO PREVENT EARLY EXTENSION

1. Friction Push Drills

These drills help train the sensation of pushing backward rather than upward during the swing.

Trail Foot Lift Drill (with a stool that slides or has wheels)

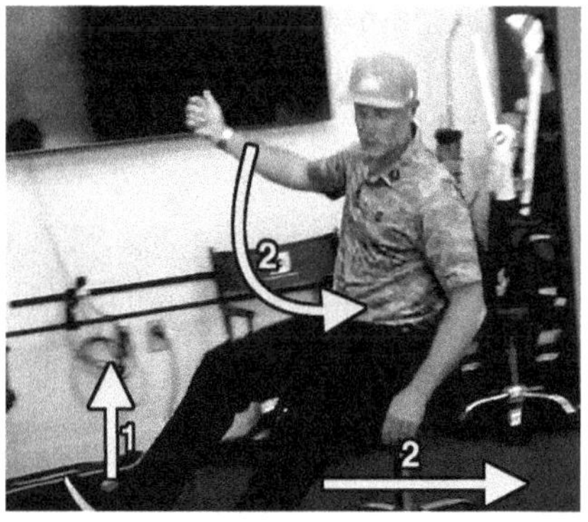

- Sit on the stool and mimic a backswing.
- While taking your hands back, lift the trail foot slightly.
- On the down swing, use your lead foot to push yourself backward in the stool as hard as you can.
    - Feel the force being put into the ball of your foot.
    - Focus on pushing back frictionally rather than moving upward.
- Progress by adding a twisting motion while pushing back.

Skateboard Drill

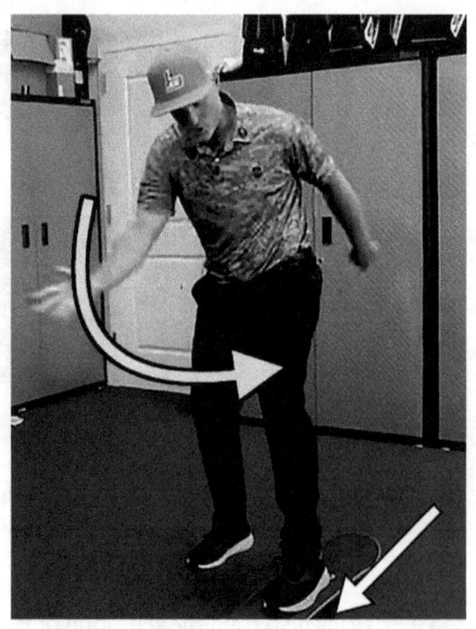

- Place a skateboard under the lead foot.
- As you transition into the downswing, push against the skateboard frictionally, not downward, moving your lead foot forward.
- Helps reinforce proper ground reaction forces in the lead foot.

Slider Drill

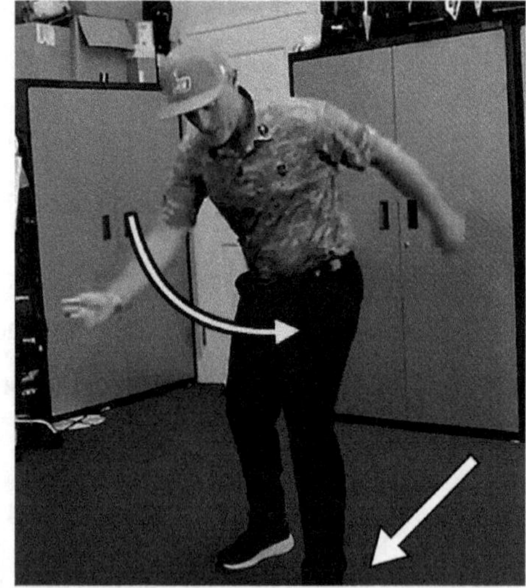

- Use a slider (like the ones at the gym) under your lead foot.
- While transitioning to the downswing, push your foot forward to train frictional push.
- BONUS: Use a flip-flop. Keep the flip-flop loose under your foot. Slide your foot into it during the transition to encourage the correct movement pattern.

2. Posture & Body Awareness Drills

These drills focus on maintaining posture and avoiding the tendency to stand up too early.

Two-Club Chest Drill

- Hold two under your arms, chest height, pointing them at the ball at setup.
- Make a swing motion. If you early extend, the clubs will point above the ball at impact.
- Proper motion keeps the tailbone back, chest down, and clubs pointing toward the ball.

Floating Ball Drill

- Hold a club across your hips, and imagine a ball floating just below your pelvis.
- Rotate to the top while keeping the ball level without letting it rise or move forward.
- In transition, feel like you are driving the ball down and left into the ground behind your lead foot.

3. Full Swing Drill

Step-Around Drill

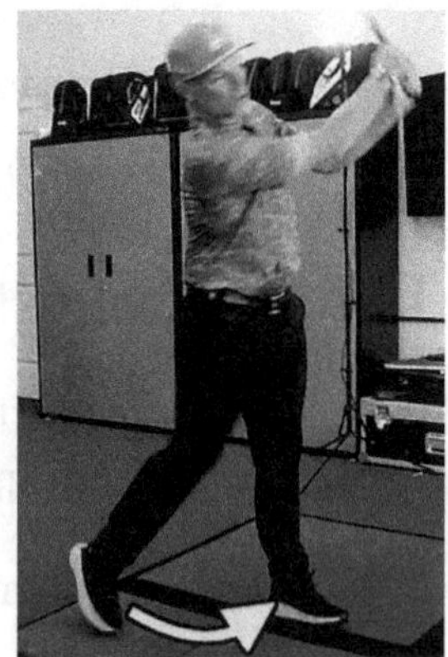

- Set up with the lead foot slightly flared open.
- Swing to the top, then push off the trail leg and step around with the lead foot to promote proper rotation.
- This prevents moving into the ball and encourages a push-and-turn motion. (Justin Rose has used this drill during practice rounds.)

- Each drill targets early extension by reinforcing ground forces, maintaining posture, and improving pelvis movement.
- Experiment to find which drill resonates best with your kinesthetic awareness.
- Repetitions and incorporating gym work can improve your effectiveness.
- The ultimate goal is to make the motion feel natural, not overly technical.

MARK BLACKBURN'S WEDGE MASTERY

See the full video here!

The secret to elite wedge play is the ability to ***hit low launch with high spin shots.***

The best players maintain the ***same amount of loft and lean on wedge shots,*** which allows them to target a two-yard distance dispersion window. That's some elite-level control to target.

Wedge Essentials

1. Low Launch, High Spin

- Target Launch Angle: 27–30°
- Low launch prevents ballooning, helping shots stop quickly. Aim for a peak height of ***50–70 feet.***
- This ensures predictability in wind and firm greens.

2. Shaft Lean & Dynamic Loft

- To get low launch, you need shaft lean.
- Shaft Lean: 15° forward at impact, delivering about 45° of loft with a 60° wedge.
- Maintain consistent dynamic loft for predictable distances across all wedges.
- This often leads to more of a draw shot.

3. Body Rotation Over Wrist Hinge

- Pro tip: Minimize wrist hinge in your backswing.
- Rotate your body through impact instead of sliding to maintain shaft lean and clean contact.
- A great example is Steve Stricker's wedge swing with minimal wrist action.

4. Three Baseline Swings

- Create three reliable swings:
    - Short swing (7:30 position)
    - Mid swing (lead arm parallel)
    - Full swing (3/4 position)

★ ***Adjust distance by changing your body rotation, not swing speed.*** ★

5. Swing Tempo & Energy

- Swing at 60–70% energy.
- ***Think of it like an underhand toss.*** It's predictable and simple.
- Swinging harder introduces inconsistencies in launch angle and spin.

6. Common Mistakes

- Swinging too hard increases unpredictable spin.
- Poor loft control leads to distance dispersion. Control the loft to control the shot.

7. Clean Contact is Crucial

- Keep your wedge grooves clean with a towel for optimal friction and spin.
- Practice off tight lies to improve your contact.

WEDGE SETUP ESSENTIALS

- **Ball Position:** Middle or slightly back in your stance.
- **Open Stance:** Slightly open stance and flare the lead foot to promote easy rotation through the ball.
- **Shaft Lean:** Start with hands slightly forward, leaning the shaft about 15° forward (one grip length).
- **Handle Height:** Slightly raise the handle to prevent excessive digging into the turf.
- **Rotation Over Slide:** Focus on rotating your body through the shot rather than sliding toward the target. This keeps your shaft lean consistent and ensures solid, clean contact.

"Great wedge play comes down to consistency in launch and spin. If you control those two factors, scoring becomes way easier." – Mark Blackburn

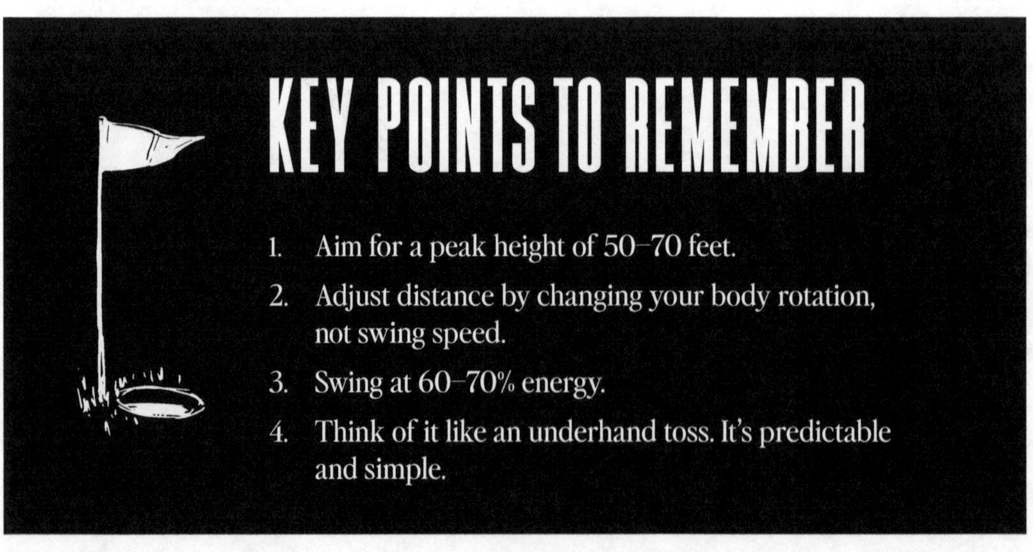

KEY POINTS TO REMEMBER

1. Aim for a peak height of 50–70 feet.
2. Adjust distance by changing your body rotation, not swing speed.
3. Swing at 60–70% energy.
4. Think of it like an underhand toss. It's predictable and simple.

Wedge Distance Tracking Table

Use this table to record your average carry distances for each wedge and swing type.

Wedge	7:30 Swing (yds)	Parallel Swing (yds)	3/4 Swing (yds)
60° (Lob Wedge)			
56° (Sand Wedge)			
50° (Gap Wedge)			
PW			

A TOUR-PROVEN, STEP-BY-STEP, PRE-ROUND ROUTINE

"Your warm-up is not a practice session – it's about getting ready to play." Your warm-up sets the tone for your round, and tour pros use it to activate their body, establish feel, and lock in mentally.

1. Activate the body for dynamic movement and speed.
2. Establish a feel for tempo, ball flight, and course conditions.
3. Mentally lock in to the competitive mindset.

Skipping this process means losing strokes before you even tee off.

Step 1: Get the body moving.

- Light cardio: Walk, jog, or cycle for 3–5 minutes.
- Dynamic mobility drills: High knees, butt kicks, lateral shuffles, torso twists.
- Power movements: Medicine ball slams, 180° jumps, resistance band activation.
    - Ensure all power movements mimic what you're working on in your swing.

Step 2: Start with wedges.

- Begin with half swings, then progress to full swings.
- Focus on strike quality and distance control.
- Pay attention to turf interaction (firm vs. soft conditions).

Step 3: Move through the bag.

- Short irons → mid irons → woods → driver
- Observe ***shot shape and dispersion,*** and don't focus on trying to make technique changes.
- Start ramping up driver speed gradually, building up to full power over several swings to feel athletic and fast.

"The goal is not to be judgmental about the shot, but objective about what's coming out (your tendencies)."

Step 4: Warm the mind up → simulate playing the course.

- Visualize and hit shots as if playing the first few holes.
- Go through a full pre-shot routine.
- Finish with an approach shot or tee shot that matches your game plan.
- We want our brains and mindsets fully warmed up.

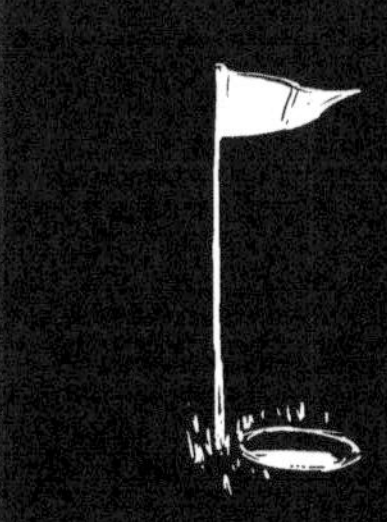

- **Warm up, don't practice. This isn't the time to fix your swing.**
- **Observe tendencies. Take notes on your shot patterns.**
- **Stay relaxed. Breathe, trust your routine, and commit to your game plan.**

THE FIVE STATS YOU'RE NOT TRACKING: SCOTT FAWCETT

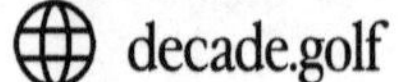

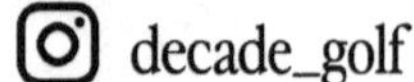

See the full video here!

Spending time learning from Scott Fawcett completely changed how I think about course strategy. His DECADE system is all about making smarter decisions that lead to lower scores.

It's the same approach that's helped countless PGA Tour and college players avoid mistakes and play their best. Once you see golf through his data-driven lens, you'll never look at the course the same way again.

The Tiger Five

The Only Stats You Need to Track to Improve Your Golf Game

We've all finished a round thinking, *I should've scored better.* But basic stats like fairways and greens don't explain where the strokes went.

That's where the "Tiger Five" come in. Scott Fawcett, creator of the DECADE system, found these mistakes are just as critical for weekend golfers as for pros.

1. Double Bogeys

Statistically, a double bogey costs 1.2 strokes compared to a bogey's 0.2 strokes.

"If you make a bogey, you're only losing a fraction of a stroke. But a double bogey? That's a full shot or more lost. Avoiding doubles is the key to shooting lower scores."

- Play smart from trouble. Instead of trying a miracle shot from the trees, punch out safely and get back into play.

2. Bogeys on Par Fives

Par fives feel like they should always be birdies, right? But did you know even PGA Tour pros average just ***4.8 strokes on these holes?***

"Golfers need to understand that laying up smartly can save strokes.
You don't always need to get as close as possible ***if it means bringing hazards into play.***"

- Most bogeys on par fives come from trying to do too much after a poor tee shot.
- If you can't reach the green in two, prioritize a ***safe layup*** that avoids trouble.
- Don't let emotions dictate your play–just because you're on a par five doesn't mean you have to force birdie.

3. Three-Putts

How many times do you blame a three-putt on a misread? The data says you probably misjudged speed!

> "If I could redo one thing, I'd obsess about speed control above all else."
> – Robert Karlsson, PGA Tour veteran

"Golfers are obsessed with making every putt, but the real goal is leaving yourself tap-ins. The moment you try to 'force' a putt in, you start making mistakes."

- Focus ***50% of putting practice*** on ***speed control drills.***
- Pace off putts to develop a feel for distance.

4. Avoiding Two-Chip Mistakes

Chipping it close feels great, but missing the green entirely can wreck your score. Too often, golfers go for the hero shot instead of the simple chip to the middle that would actually save strokes.

Scott explains, "Your first goal is to get the ball on the green. If you miss the green twice, you've made an unforced error that costs you big time."

- If you're more yards off the green than the pin is on, ***play conservatively.***
- Don't let frustration cause compounding mistakes.

5. Bogeys Inside 150 Yards

Tiger's greatest scoring leap came from nearly eliminating bogeys within 150 yards. The common mistake? Trying too hard to hit it close and aiming at pins.

Golf isn't about perfection – it's about minimizing mistakes. ***Expectation management, not aggression, leads to lower scores.***

Scott pointed out, "Tiger wasn't suddenly better at golf. He just stopped making dumb mistakes with short irons."

- If you're making bogeys inside 150 yards, you're being ***too aggressive.***
- Most golfers score lower by ***avoiding mistakes,*** not making more birdies.
- Expectation management is key – don't let frustration lead to forced shots.

Use the "Tiger Five" Round Tracker on the next page to start tracking these stats and make smarter decisions on the course!

THE TIGER FIVE ROUND TRACKER

Round #	Bogey on Par 5	Double Bogey	Three-Putt	Bogey Inside 150 Yards	Two-Chip Hole	Total
1						
2						
3						
4						
5						
6						
7						
8						
9						
10						

- After each round, add tally marks in the boxes for each mistake you made.
- Tiger Woods aimed to keep these mistakes to ***six or fewer per tournament*** – which meant fewer than 1.5 per round. For amateur golfers, a realistic goal is to ***keep your total under six per round*** to start seeing improvements.

How to Avoid the Mental Traps That Lead to Bogeys

★ Ditch the "I-Should-Make-Birdie-Here" mentality. Many bogeys happen because golfers force aggressive shots when they should be playing smart.

★ Practice patience. If you're out of position, don't try to hero your way out – play for bogey at worst, not double.

★ Think in fractions of shots. Not every shot needs to be perfect. A safe play now saves multiple strokes over 18 holes.

★ Control your emotions. A frustrated bogey often leads to a reckless mistake on the next hole. Keep your cool.

★ Visualize conservative targets. More middle-of-the-green shots mean fewer flag-hunting disasters.

Reducing bogeys isn't about hitting better shots. It's about making smarter decisions. Play within your limits, avoid unnecessary risks, and let the good scores come to you.

STOP GUESSING WITH RALPH BAUER'S ULTIMATE GREEN READING PROCESS

Download the app: tourreadgolf.com

ralphbauergolf

See the full video here!

Ralph Bauer was in town for the 3M Open, coaching some of the best tour players in the world, and I got the chance to learn from him firsthand. He teaches a green reading system that takes the guesswork out of putting. It's simple, it's practical, and you can start using it your next time out.

Start with the skill of hitting your start line.

"Can you make a straight 5-footer?"

That's the first question Ralph asks. Because if you can't hit your start line, no green reading system in the world is going to help you.

He recommends practicing with a putting mirror on a straight putt. Once you can consistently roll it on line, you're ready to move on to reading break.

Tour players make 90% of putts from 12 feet in a controlled start-line test. But their on-course make rate is only 30%. That means 60% of the equation is speed and green reading.

Understand the variables before you calculate break.

Before you start reading greens, you have to have a rough idea of the variables that affect break:

- The slope (% of slope on the green)
- The length of the putt (count paces)
- The green speed (stimp rating)

Do the math *(there's an easy formula).*

Ralph uses a formula to predict how much a putt will break based on length and slope:

Number of Paces × 2 - 1 = inches of break (on a 1% slope)

**This is based on a green rolling at a 10 on the stimp 12 inches past the hole*

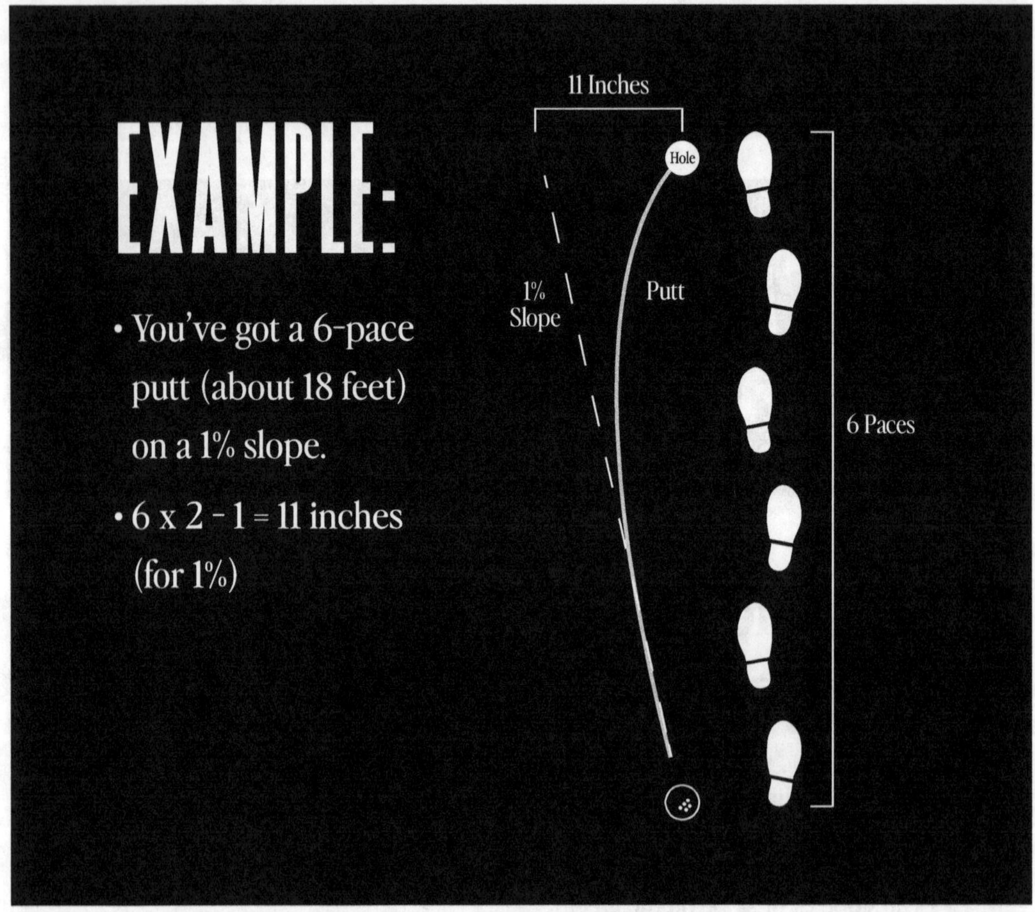

Match speed and line using the clock system.

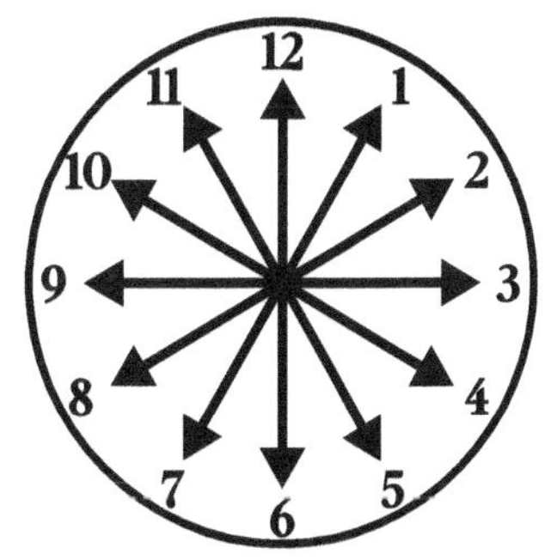

The clock system

Next, you need to figure out how speed affects the break. Ralph teaches golfers to imagine a clock over the cup. If your putt breaks 16 inches left, it's not going in at 6 o'clock.

You have to visualize where the ball is going to enter the hole, then build your line and speed around that. Tour players spend 3-4 seconds visualizing every putt. They see the entry point, feel the pace, and ***commit***.

Don't just fall in love with your start line. ***Fall in love with the whole putt.***

Have questions?

Learn the whole system by signing up for Ralph's app here:

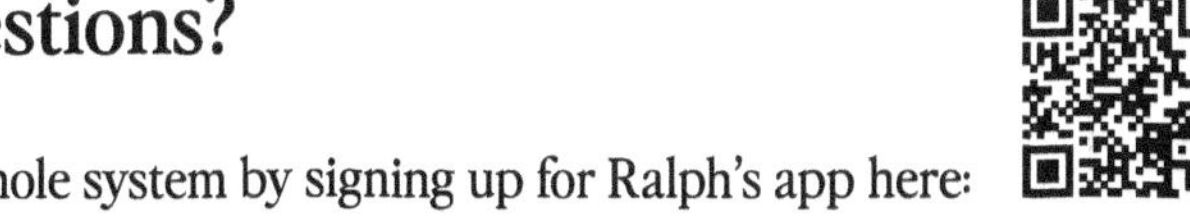

THE FACTS OF GREEN READING

1. ***Always read from the low point looking uphill.*** Ralph found that the most accurate reads come from halfway between the ball and the hole, ***looking uphill.*** Looking downhill makes the slope appear 25% flatter.
2. ***If you're not sure which way it's breaking, try the "1-foot test":*** look one foot above and one foot below the line and ask yourself, "What's higher?"
3. ***Visualize the putt for 3-4 seconds.*** Every great putter Ralph has worked with takes time to visualize the putt's path, especially how it enters the hole. It helps blend start line, speed, and entry point into one picture.
4. ***Use a line on the ball.*** Ralph encourages all his players to use one. It helps align your start line precisely, builds confidence, and keeps your focus on where the putt needs to start, even on long or tricky putts.

THE MAKING OF A PRO: DYLAN WU

dylan_wu59

See the full video here! ←

Dylan Wu grew up in Southern Oregon, where every round with his brothers was a competition. By his early teens, he was one of the top junior players in the state, dominating local events and proving he had the talent to go far.

That early success led him to Northwestern University, where he refined his game. His path to the PGA Tour was a grind – through PGA Tour Canada, Korn Ferry Tour Q-School, and a breakthrough win at the 2021 Price Cutter Charity Championship, which secured his PGA Tour card.

Key Mindset Shifts from Junior Golf to the PGA Tour

At 15, Dylan Wu was one of Oregon's top junior golfers, but at the Wyndham Cup, he found himself competing against future PGA Tour stars Sam Burns and Scottie Scheffler. For the first time, he wasn't the best player on the course, and that felt different.

What set them apart wasn't their swing but their *mindset.* They shrugged off mistakes, stayed calm under pressure, and ***never let a bad shot define their round.***

1. Redefining a "good" shot

- As a junior, Dylan thought you had to stuff it ***inside 10 feet*** to be elite.
- "The one thing people don't realize is that pros don't hit it as close as you think. You see Rory or Tiger land it like a feather, but most of the time, we're just trying to get it on the green and in the right spot."
- It's about smart targets and giving yourself makeable pars and occasional birdies.

2. You're competing against yourself, not others.

- Wu learned to ***stop worrying about how other players looked in practice.***
- "I remember playing with Sam Burns and Scottie Scheffler at 15 and thinking, 'These guys are so good.' You can't focus on that. You have to just focus on what you do best."
- You have to focus on ***executing your own game plan*** and not worry about what someone else is doing.

3. Mental toughness is more important than mechanics.

- Handling ***bad shots without emotional spirals*** is a skill that separates top players.

- Learn to ***accept the occasional bad round*** and stay committed to long-term goals.
- "The biggest thing I'd tell my younger self? Stop living and dying by every shot. I used to mutter to myself [and] get mad at every mistake. That stuff only holds you back."

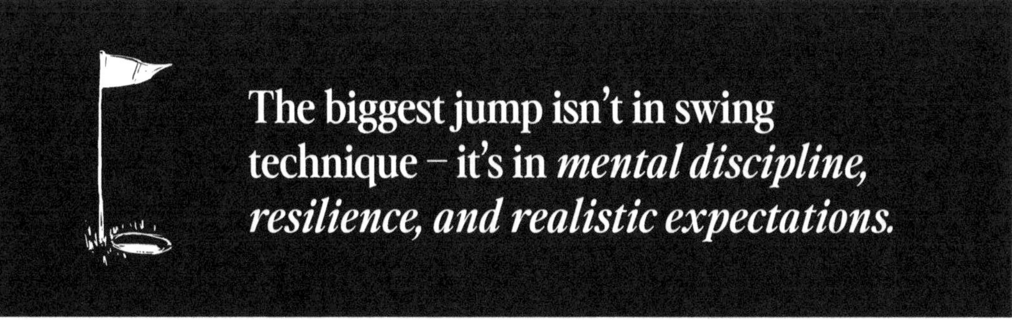

Course Strategy: How Pros Manage Risk & Reward

The first time Wu played a full season as a pro, he realized ***elite golf was more about managing misses*** than hitting great shots. In college, he aimed at every flag, but on tougher setups, that approach led to short-sided misses and unnecessary bogeys.

1. Why hitting it to 20–24 feet is the best choice:

- Most amateurs think pros hit every iron inside 10 feet.
- The reality is that a ***shot within 20 feet from 150–175 yards is incredible.***
- Wu plays to maximize greens in regulation, not to chase flags.
- "If I have a 5-iron, I'm aiming for the fat part of the green. I'm not going at the flag unless it's perfect."

2. The decision-making framework Wu uses:

- Green light: Perfect number and little danger – ***attack the flag.***
- Yellow light: Slight risk and mid-range number – ***play for the middle of the green.***
- Red light: Tough pin and hazards in play – ***play safe side and two-putt.***
- "If I'm feeling great, maybe I''ll aim five feet closer to the pin, but I'm never just firing at every flag.

3. Smart targets: Where to aim on approach shots:

- Short irons: Can be aggressive, but always factor in ***spin and slope.***
- Mid irons: Play for ***safety zones,*** avoiding ***short-sided misses.***
- Long irons: The goal is ***center green, two-putt, and move on.***
- "I'd rather be 25 feet away with a putt than short-sided in a bunker with no chance."

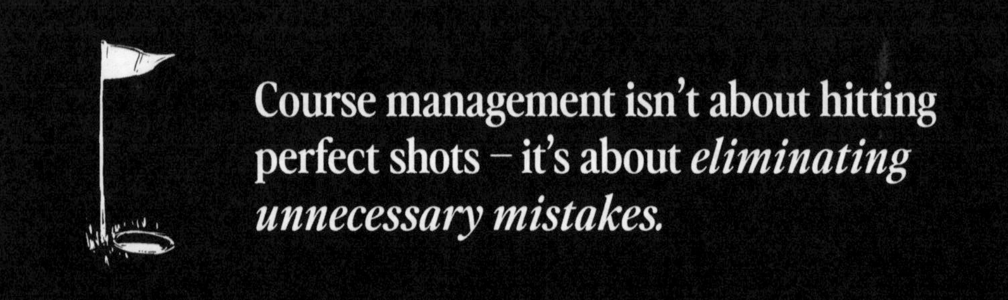

Course management isn't about hitting perfect shots – it's about *eliminating unnecessary mistakes.*

DR. LUKE BENOIT: HOW TO MAKE A SWING CHANGE USING FOAM GOLF BALLS

rypgolf.com

dr.luke.benoit.golf

See the full video here!

Swing changes are hard, and the way we've been taught to change hasn't made it any easier. The key is to focus on learning a new movement pattern first, rather than hitting great shots right away.

"You have to slow down and exaggerate the new movement," Luke explains. Luke Benoit is at the cutting edge of motor learning research, consistently innovating practical ideas that genuinely transform golfers' swings.

That's why he's become a huge believer in one of the simplest tools around: ***foam golf balls.***

No temptation to chase good contact. Only pure reps focused on movement.

"If you can make it look right with a foam ball," Luke says, "you're way more likely to get it to stick with a real one."

- Prioritize movement quality over ball contact.
- Foam balls remove the pressure of making perfect shots.
- Slowly integrate your new swing into actual play.
- Be patient. Swing changes take time but are SO worth it!

THE SWING CHANGE PROCESS

Step One: Freezer Swings – No Ball

Go to the top, freeze, then swing, and stay focused on the movement.

Step Two: Slow Backswing – No Ball

Add a slow three-second backswing, then fire into the downswing.

Step Three: Freezer Swing – Foam Ball

Do the same freezer drill, but now hit a foam ball. Expect bad shots; just don't repeat the same contact miss twice.

Step Four: Slow Backswing – Foam Ball

Now add a three-second backswing with the foam ball.

Step Five: Alternate Freezer + Slow Backswing

Keep switching between the two drills to make sure the movement is perfect.

Step Six: Add a Real Ball

Once the foam ball swing looks 95% of the way there (and contact's improving), it's time. But you'll keep alternating between freezer and slow backswing with real balls, too.

Step 1: Freezers, the Motor Learning Hack

Most sports involve open-loop learning (a.k.a. reacting in real-time, like shooting a basketball). Golf, though, is more closed-loop, so you have time to prepare and adjust.

Freezers combine both: You freeze (closed-loop: time to think), then fire into your swing (open-loop: full commitment). This trains your brain faster than just hitting ball after ball.

It's simple: ***swing to the top and stop.*** Pause. Feel the position and have all your swing thoughts and changes top of mind. Then, ***fire into the downswing at full speed.***

How to Do the Freezer Drill (No Ball)

1. Take the club to the top and freeze. Hold it there.
2. Exaggerate your swing change – whether that's more hip turn, better shallowing, or keeping space between the arms and chest.
3. Rehearse the downswing slowly. Keep your trail arm wide and externally rotated, the club shallowing behind you, and your chest rotating and lowering into the ground.
4. ***Think about everything*** – this is where you overload the brain. That's good. You're building a new blueprint.
5. Repeat without a ball until the move looks 95% right on camera.

"You don't need to hit a single ball to get better at your swing. ***You need to learn the movement first."***

Step 2: Slow Backswing, Full-Speed Downswing

Once you've got the freezer move down, it's time to blend in some flow.

"A lot of people try to change their swing at full speed, and it just doesn't work. So we slow down the backswing to give the brain more time to organize the downswing." This bridges the gap between slow rehearsals and real golf swings.

3-Second Backswing

1. Count "1-2-3" as you take the club back slowly.
2. At the top, trigger the downswing with speed.
3. Alternate with freezer drills so the move stays clean.
4. Record your swing. Watch for the move, not contact.

"People who only do freezer drills end up with two swings: their drill swing, and their real one. You need both the structure and the motion."

Step 3: Add a Foam Golf Ball

Here's where the magic happens. Most golfers panic when they hit a bad shot and instantly revert to old habits. Foam balls remove that feedback loop. "The goal isn't to hit a perfect shot," Luke says. "It's to make the swing look right."

Expect mishits; thin, fat, toe, heel. The only rule is to ***not make the same mistake twice.***

Movement with Foam Balls

1. Start with freezer swings using a foam ball.
2. Add in slow backswing swings with foam balls.
3. Track your misses, but stay focused on swing mechanics, not outcomes.
4. Video your swing: aim for 95% perfection in how it looks, not how it flies.

"The worse you hit it, the better your swing changes are going to get. Just don't miss the same way twice."

Step 4: Transition to a Real Golf Ball

This is where most people revert back to their original swings. They go straight from drills to real balls and expect magic. But the second you introduce a real ball, your brain flips back into performance mode.

"You're not ready for a real ball until the foam ball swing looks 95% correct," Luke says. "If it doesn't look good with a foam ball, it won't magically look good with a real one."

Real Ball Transition Plan

1. Continue alternating freezer and slow-backswing swings.
2. Start with block practice: same shot, same target, same club.
3. If you lose the feel? Go back to foam. Re-groove it.
4. Track your swing on video, not ball flight.

Step 5: Taking It to the Course

The Two-Swing Approach

"You're building a new house, but you don't have to live in it yet," Luke says.

"You can still play rounds using your old swing while you continue building the new one."

You don't have to throw yourself into tournament play with a brand-new swing. In fact, it's better if you don't. Luke calls this the bifurcated model: Play with the old swing. Practice the new one. And let them merge over time.

Wrapping Up

Most people never successfully change their swing – not because they lack discipline, but because they ***lack a process.***

This ***IS*** the process. And foam balls might be your biggest secret weapon.

I've worked with a lot of coaches and tried a lot of training tools, but this one hit different. Watching Luke walk through this step-by-step made something click for me.

I realized I've been rushing it. Trying to go straight from concept to perfect contact. ***But every time I forced a change at full speed, it crumbled.***

My big takeaway is this: It's not about hitting great shots right away. It's about building a swing that holds up under pressure, one layer at a time.

So if you're working on a change, don't just grind harder. Slow it down. Break it apart. Use foam balls. Use video. Use this progression.

And give yourself a chance to actually change.

WHY THE FOAM BALL METHOD WORKS: THE SCIENCE BEHIND SWING CHANGES

In 1967, psychologists Paul Fitts and Michael Posner identified three key stages every golfer goes through when learning a new movement:

1. **Cognitive** – Figuring out what to do.
2. **Associative** – Figuring out how to do it consistently.
3. **Autonomous** – Doing it automatically, even under pressure.

Here's why Luke Benoit's swing-change method aligns perfectly with this science – and why the foam ball approach makes so much sense.

Stage 1: Cognitive (Learning What the Swing Looks Like)

When you first try a new swing, your brain is just trying to understand it:

- Where should the club go?
- What positions am I aiming for?
- How does this new swing differ from my old one?

In this stage, it's critical to get clear, visual feedback. That's why the early steps of Luke's method involve no ball at all – just making exaggerated movements, using video feedback, and consciously processing what the swing should look like.

Here's why this method aligns: Removing the ball at first means zero pressure to hit a perfect shot. Using video helps you clearly understand exactly what you're aiming to achieve – allowing your brain to build a strong mental blueprint.

"You can't build a new swing until your brain fully understands what the correct movement actually looks like. That's why video feedback, without any ball, is key."

Stage 2: Associative (Making the Swing Reliable)

Once you've clearly understood the new swing, your focus shifts to repeating it consistently. At this stage, making mistakes is beneficial – it helps your brain pinpoint precisely what adjustments need to be made.

This is where foam balls enter the picture. Foam balls provide instant feedback without harsh consequences for poor shots. You can safely experiment, fail, adjust, and repeat until the swing feels natural.

"If you aren't comfortable hitting some ugly shots along the way, you're not truly changing anything. Foam balls help you safely embrace that messy learning stage."

Stage 3: Autonomous (Swinging Automatically Under Pressure)

Eventually, after enough mindful repetition, the new swing becomes automatic. You no longer think; you swing confidently, even under stress.

Most golfers stumble because they rush straight from the initial cognitive stage to competition, skipping essential associative practice. That's like learning basic guitar chords today and trying to perform on stage tomorrow.

Foam balls bridge the gap, gradually easing you from slow-motion drills (with no ball) to low-pressure swings (with foam balls) and finally to real ball performance. This progression ensures the new swing pattern ***sticks when it counts.***

"You can't shortcut real learning. This structured progression is exactly what your brain needs to make a lasting swing change." – Dr. Luke Benoit

BALL STRIKING DRILLS FOR EVERY PLAYER

For 20 Handicaps: Low Point Control Drill

1. Mark a line on the ground using spray chalk, foot powder, or a club.
2. Place a row of balls on the line and hit each one, paying attention to:
    - Where the divot starts (it should be after the ball).
    - The direction of the divot (should be slightly left for a straight shot).
3. Adjust your swing based on what you see.

Important Adjustments:

- If the divot is too far behind → Shift weight forward.
- If the divot is too far in front → Check ball position and release timing.
- If the divot points way left or right → Adjust clubface or swing path.
- **Your goal:** Hit ten shots and get at least seven divots in the right spot before moving on.

For 10 Handicaps: Shot Shaping Challenge

Train your ability to hit draws, fades, and straight shots on command. Even though you might feel like this is too challenging for your skill, this awareness of shot shape will help you understand your miss and why it's happening.

1. Set an alignment stick on the ground pointing at your target.
2. Choose your shot shape before each swing:
    - **Draw:** Aim feet right, slightly close the clubface.
    - **Fade:** Aim feet left, slightly open the clubface.
    - **Straight:** Square stance and face.
3. Grade your shot based on how close it was to the intended shape.
4. Rotate through Draw → Straight → Fade, and adjust accordingly.

Important Adjustments:

- If the ball isn't curving enough, exaggerate the clubface adjustment.
- If the ball over-curves, reduce the face adjustment.
- **Your goal:** Hit five correct shots of each shape before finishing.

For 0 Handicaps: The Ultimate Ball Striking Test

Test your ability to control distance, shape, and ball flight.

1. Generate a random carry number between 100-250 yards (use an app or dice).
2. Hit 18 shots following this shot sequence:
    - Normal → Draw → Normal → Fade → Normal → Wind-Controlled (low flight)
3. Score yourself on each shot based on how close you are to the carry yardage:
    - Eagle: Within 1 yard
    - Birdie: 1 4 yards
    - Par: 4-7 yards
    - Bogey: 7-10 yards
    - Double Bogey: 10+ yards
4. If you don't match the correct shot shape, take a penalty stroke on your score.

Hit 20 shots and log your score. Do this regularly, and see how your ball striking is improving!

Yardage Range: ____ yds to ____ yds

Attempt	1	2	3	4	5	6	7	8	9	10	Total
Score											

JON SINCLAIR: SHOULD YOU HIT 30-YARD WEDGES STEEP OR SHALLOW?

sinclairgolf.com

jonsinclairgolf

See the full video here!

Should you be steep or shallow on your wedge shots? A lot of coaches have strong opinions, but Jon Sinclair has something better... ***data.***

Jon tracked hundreds of wedge shots from top-50 players in the world and looked at what the players themselves said were their "good" shots.

Here's what the data showed on those 30-yarders:

- Launch Angle: Always between 27-30°
- Players who drifted above that fell out of the top 50 in wedge play.
- When they got back in, launch angle dropped back to 27-30°.

Jon's theory: Landing angle might matter even more than launch.

Here's why steeper usually wins (especially on tight lies):

- **Shallow:** Attack angle 0° to -5° down
- **Medium:** 6°-10° down
- **Steep:** 10°+ down

If you're coming in too shallow, say 5° down, you're more likely to catch the grass first. If you see a "grass badge" on your wedge after hitting a shot that felt "clipped," this might be the case.

Ping found that 86% of wedge shots hit the ground before the ball – and that's probably not helping you chip it closer.

So what gives you the best chance to still hit it clean? ***Get steeper.*** You're pushing the grass down, not dragging it up the face.

Here's how to get steeper (without screwing everything up):

Here's the easiest three-second tip Jon gave me:

"Move your center forward an inch on takeaway, pelvis, chest, and head. Just shift forward."

That slight move shifts your low point forward and gets you more down on the ball without changing ball position or getting weird with your hands.

And to keep it spinning, you still need dynamic loft around 45° (not leaning too much). That means keeping a ***forward body position*** while still trying to ***hit it high.***

Sounds backwards, but it works.

Go forward. Then hit it high.

Add speed. *Don't* be careful.

Here's why this is so important: spin is primarily created by friction, and friction comes from ***spin loft*** and ***clubhead speed.***

Spin loft is the difference between your dynamic loft and attack angle. If that window is too small, you won't generate enough spin. But if you don't have enough speed, even the ideal spin loft won't produce the friction you need.

So when Jon says "spin comes from speed," he means you need to ***swing with confidence.*** Babying the shot kills the friction window.

Jon said something that hit home: "When I chipped the best, I felt aggressive. Not careful."

You can't baby these shots and expect zip. Feel like you're "striking a match," like Gary Player used to say. Brush the ground with a confident, snappy strike.

Your wedge shot checklist (30 yards):

- ☐ **Ideal Launch Angle:** 27–30°
- ☐ **Dynamic Loft:** ~45°
- ☐ **Attack Angle:** 7–10° down (medium to steep)
- ☐ **Spin Loft:** 50–55°
- ☐ **Ball Spin:** 6,000+ rpm
- ☐ **Clubhead Speed:** ~43 mph
- ☐ **Feel:** Go forward, hit it high, strike the match.

WILL ROBINS'S FIVE HABITS TO ACTUALLY LOWER YOUR SCORES

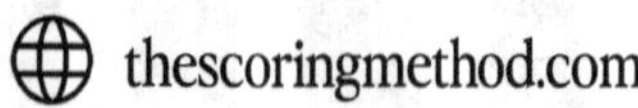
thescoringmethod.com

willrobinspga

See the full video here!

I always enjoy learning from Coach Will Robins because he's someone who helps you get better with the swing and game you have today. After spending a couple of days filming and playing golf together, he gave me five things to work on going forward. Here's what he shared and why it might help you too.

1. Start with a go-to club.

Problem: You bomb the driver one day... and the next day might not be able to hit a fairway.

Fix: Have a reliable fairway finder when you're not feeling it. No one has their driver dialed and ready to go every day you need to have another go-to shot ready.

What Will Recommends

1. Choose a go-to club (for example, a 2-iron, 5-wood, or hybrid).
2. Relentlessly practice hitting it into a 30-yard fairway on the range.
3. Know when to bench the driver (for example, a tight tee shot, the first few holes, etc).

2. Know your yardages!

Problem: It feels like everything goes the same distance, and there's no clarity on what yardages your clubs go.

Fix: Chart your yardages for ***every*** swing: 9:00 swing, 3/4, full, smash. Build out a matrix of distances for each iron.

What Will Recommends:

1. Use a launch monitor to get data and record 10 shots each: 9:00 swing, 3/4, full, smash.
2. Create a personal yardage chart for each club.

3. Master the wedge clock system.

Problem: You're launching wedges to the moon and guessing on distances.

Fix: Train your body to deliver consistent swing lengths like 9:00, 10:30, and full. Combine this with tempo and launch angle control to hit specific yardages from 50–120 yards.

Drill: The Clock System Ladder

- Pick one wedge.
- Hit three shots each at 9:00, 10:30, and full swings.
- Chart distance + ball flight.
- Switch clubs and repeat.

4. Expand Your Chipping Arsenal

Problem: You're addicted to the lob wedge.

Fix: Practice chipping with multiple clubs (9-iron, PW, SW, LW) to understand rollout and landing zones. It's not always about spinning it close; sometimes it's about playing the easy shot that has the highest percentage of getting within eight feet of the hole.

What Will Recommends:

- Practice chips with at least four clubs.
- Learn where each lands and how it rolls out.
- Use lower-lofted clubs when possible for simplicity and control.

"You don't need Phil-level touch – just more options."

5. Train Putts from 6 to 15 Feet

Problem: You're solid inside four feet, but the make percentage goes downhill from 8-12 feet.

Fix: Use games like the 10-Point Putting Game to challenge yourself under pressure and build consistency at scoring distances.

DR. SASHO MACKENZIE: THE IMPORTANCE OF FACE-TO-PATH VARIABILITY

thestacksystem.com

sashomackenzie

Listen to the podcast episode here!

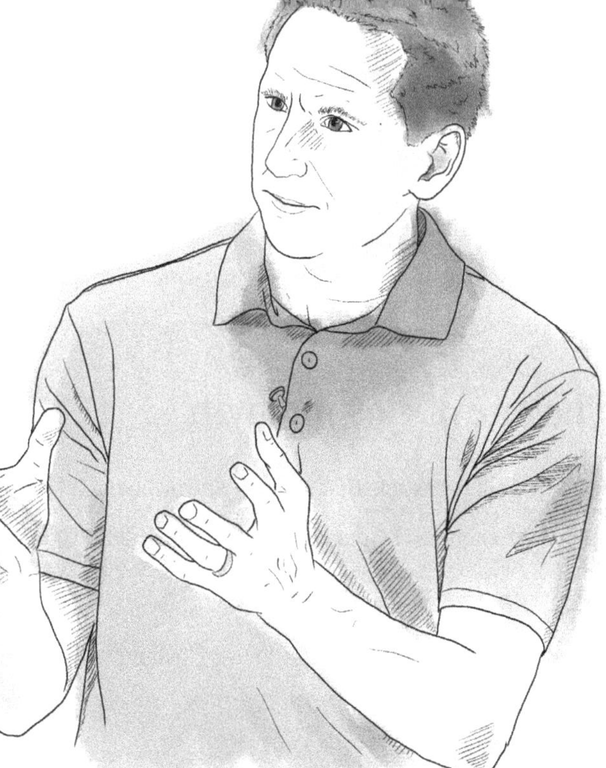

I always like to keep up to date on golf research, and no one is more on top of it than Dr. Sasho MacKenzie. He's one of the top biomechanists in golf and co-founder of the Stack.

I caught up with him after the 2024 World Scientific of Golf and learned about a workshop he did on a fascinating topic.

Face-to-path variability measures how consistently a player delivers the clubface relative to the swing path at impact. It's the number that controls both start direction and curvature. When it changes from swing to swing, dispersion increases. When it stays tight, the ball flight is repeatable.

"When you look at good players versus great players, the separator isn't speed or mechanics," Sasho said. "It's face-to-path variability." ***The path tends to stay fairly stable, especially for good players. The face is what moves. And that movement explains most inconsistencies in start line and curve.***

"Path variability is usually very small," Sasho explained. "The face is much more variable, and that's what drives dispersion."

How to measure it

During his workshop at the 2024 World Scientific Congress of Golf, Sasho described a simple way to evaluate this: have a player hit a stock shot, then hit other types of shots in between (like a putt or chip) and come back to the same stock shot again. Track how closely the face-to-path numbers match from swing to swing.

"You want to see how well a player can reproduce that same face-to-path relationship," he said. "If you're trying to hit one specific shot and that number keeps moving around, you can't control start line or curvature."

A good launch monitor will show face angle, path, and a standard deviation across all your shots. According to Sasho, elite players tend to stay under two degrees of face-to-path variability.

The rate of closure myth

Many golfers assume that slowing down the rate of face rotation through impact creates more consistency. The data doesn't support that idea.

"You can have a really high rate of closure and still have extremely low face-to-path variability," Sasho said. "Phil Mickelson and Victor Hovland couldn't be more different mechanically, but both deliver the face consistently."

He's found that rate of closure has no strong correlation with performance or variability. A faster or slower face rotation doesn't determine who strikes it best. What matters is how repeatable the motion is.

Try This Drill to Assess and Improve Face-to-Path Variability.

Setup

On the range, select a target distance and use a mid-iron (like a 7- or 8-iron).Focus on hitting your stock shot shape, whether it's a draw or a fade.

Execution

Hit 10 shots, focusing on replicating the same shot each time. Between each shot, perform another task like hitting a putt or taking a short walk to simulate in-game conditions. This helps replicate the variability you might experience during an actual round.

Measurement

Use a launch monitor to record the face-to-path data for each shot. The goal is to minimize the variability in these measurements.

What Is a Good Result?

According to Sasho, a ***"good" face-to-path variability is typically under two degrees.*** He adds that for those aiming to be "super elite," you would want your face-to-path variability to be so low that it's within the "fuzz of the machine," meaning it's approaching the limits of what the launch monitor can accurately measure.

FIELD EXPERIMENT: FACE-TO-PATH VARIABILITY CHALLENGE: FIND YOUR GO-TO SHOT.

- **Select Three Shot Shapes:** Draw, straight, and fade.
- **Hit Five Shots of Each:** Record the face-to-path variability for each set.
- **Analyze:** Determine which shot shape has the lowest variability and consider making that your go-to shot under pressure.

By focusing on reducing your face-to-path variability through these drills, you can gain greater control over your ball flight, improve your consistency on the course, and ultimately lower your scores.

IS YOUR GRIP RUINING YOUR SWING? WITH LIAM MUCKLOW

mygolflab.ca

liammucklow

See the full video here!

If you want to learn about some of the most interesting tech and research advancements in golf, you talk to Liam Mucklow. He's been leading the way in motion capture, club data, and performance analysis for years, connecting research with real-world coaching.

We've all heard it before: "Grip the club like it's a bird – tight enough to hold on but gentle enough not to crush it." It sounds wise and poetic, like something passed down from a legend of the game. ***But is that actually good advice?***

What Is Grip Strength?

Grip strength is how much force your hands can squeeze or hold onto something.

Grip strength is measured using a tool called a dynamometer (see right). It's a small device you hold in your hand and squeeze as hard as you can. You test each hand separately and add both hands together to find your total grip strength.

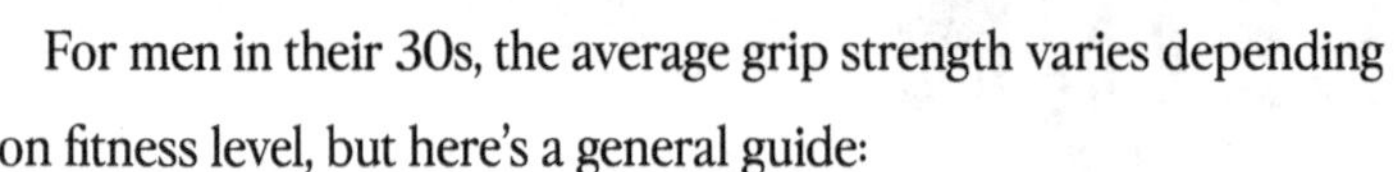

For men in their 30s, the average grip strength varies depending on fitness level, but here's a general guide:

- **Dominant Hand:** Around 105–125 pounds
- **Non-Dominant Hand:** Slightly lower, usually around 95–115 pounds
- **Combined Strength (both hands):** About 200–250 pounds

If your grip strength is over 130 pounds per hand, you're in the strong-to-elite range. The pros in Liam's study averaged 276 pounds total grip strength between both hands; that's roughly 138 pounds per hand.

So we start out with the understanding that these guys have ***elite*** level grip strength. Maybe it's from strength training in the gym or the decades of hitting golf balls at high level of speeds.

What Did the Study Reveal About Grip Strength in Golf?

After they measured the initial grip strength using a dynamometer, they had each golfer hit shots with a club that had a SensorEdge Sensor Grip installed, a specialized golf club grip embedded with pressure sensors. This technology captures real-time data on the pressure exerted by each hand throughout the swing, providing detailed insights into grip dynamics.

Who Was in the Study?

	Avg. Age	Combined Grip Strength	Avg. Differential
Pros	29.7	276 lbs	13.4 lbs
Hookers	42	252 lbs	4.4 lbs
Slicers	42.7	193 lbs	-5.1 lbs
High Handicappers	50	147 lbs	-7.3 lbs

Let's get into the data!

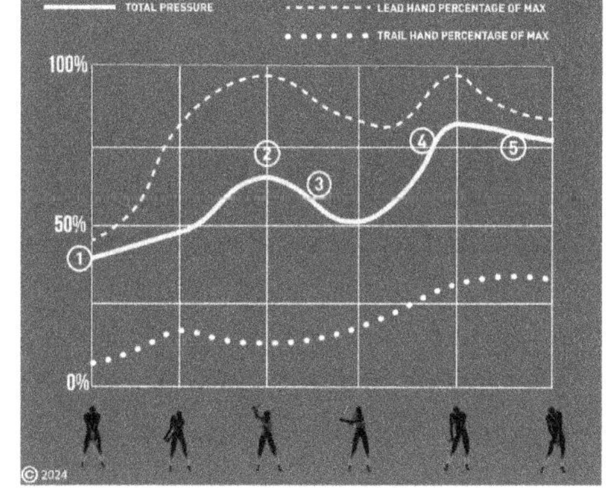

1. **Setup:** Grip pressure starts firm (around 40-50% of max strength). Based on their elite level grip strength to begin with, this is a pretty strong grip.
2. **Backswing:** Pressure remains steady throughout the backswing.
3. **Transition:** There's a slight dip in grip pressure during the transition from backswing to downswing. Liam explained that this small release allows the club to naturally "fall behind" and sync with the rotation of the body – a key move for creating lag and setting up an efficient downswing.
4. **Impact:** Grip pressure ramps up naturally as the club accelerates, ensuring stability at the moment of contact. This even increase in pressure likely minimizes clubface rotation and maximizes energy transfer to the ball.

What's Happening:

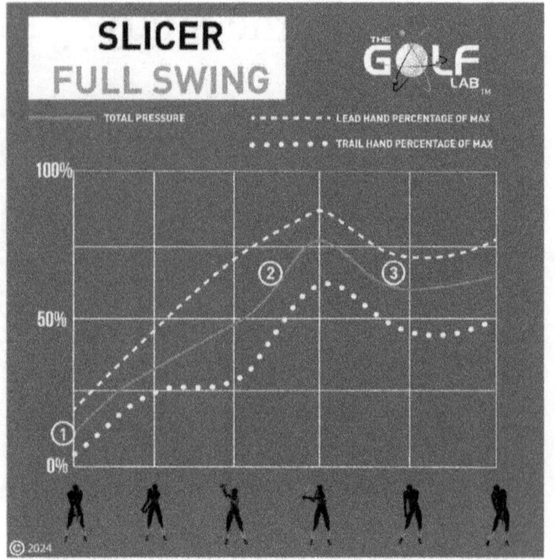

1. **Setup:** Slicers typically start with a grip pressure that's too light, often below 20% of max strength.
2. **Backswing:** Grip pressure builds unevenly, with the trail hand applying too much pressure compared to the lead hand.
3. **Transition:** The trail hand pressure spikes early in the downswing. This push from the trail hand throws the club onto an out-to-in path, creating the classic over-the-top move.
4. **Impact:** The trail hand dominates at impact, and the lead hand isn't able to stabilize the clubface. This lack of balance leaves the clubface open, causing the ball to slice to the right.

What's Happening:

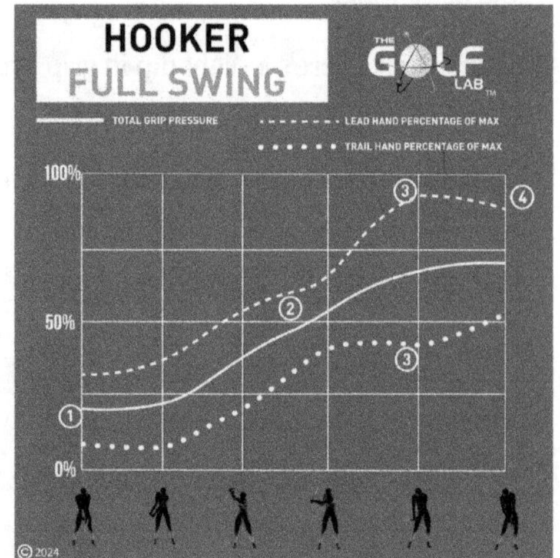

1. **Setup:** Hookers generally have a better grip pressure than slicers, but it's still not perfect. They tend to favor their lead hand too much at the start, which sets up an imbalance.
2. **Backswing:** The lead hand gradually increases pressure, while the trail hand stays under-engaged. Liam pointed out that this can cause the club to lag too far behind the body, especially when combined with a lack of rotation.
3. **Transition:** Lead hand pressure spikes during the transition as hookers try to "pull" the club through the swing. Without proper hip rotation, this extra lead hand pressure causes the club to drop behind them and swing too far from the inside.
4. **Impact:** The trail hand tries to correct by closing the clubface aggressively, resulting in a big hook. This overcorrection is common for players who rely too much on their hands to fix their swing path.

What's Happening:

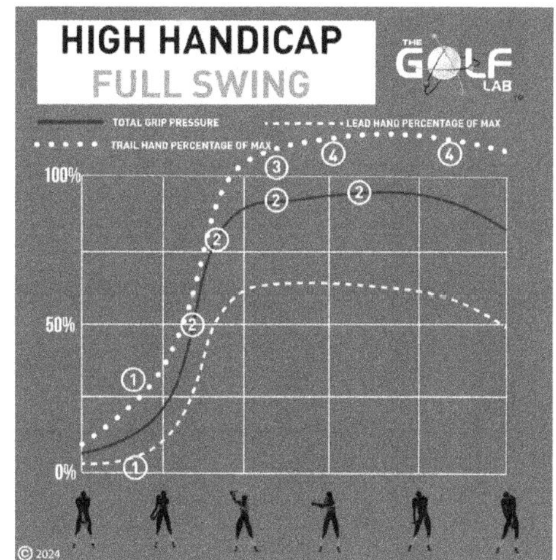

1. Setup: High handicappers grip the club extremely lightly at setup, often under 10% of max grip strength. It creates instability and a lack of control before the swing even starts.

2. Backswing: Grip pressure remains low throughout the backswing, showing a lack of engagement and control. Liam described this as amateurs "letting the club swing them," rather than taking control of the swing themselves.

3. Transition: During the downswing, there's a sudden spike in grip pressure, especially in the trail hand as they start to "hang on for dear life," as the club moves out of sync with the body, forcing the player to react instead of staying in control.

4. Impact: Both hands max out their grip pressure just before impact, but it's uncoordinated. This kind of reactive pressure spike leads to inconsistent contact and energy leaks, as the clubface twists instead of staying stable.

So what's happening and why?

1. **Pro Players:** Start with firm grip pressure, maintain consistency, and lighten during transition to shallow and sync the club with body rotation.
2. **Slicers:** Grip too lightly at setup, overuse the trail hand in transition, and push the club into an out-to-in path, leaving the face open.
3. **Hookers:** Over-rely on the lead hand, spike pressure in transition, and lack rotation, causing the club to lag too far behind and close too aggressively.
4. **High Handicappers:** Grip too lightly at setup, lose control during the swing, and reactively spike pressure with the trail hand, leading to inconsistency.

SPEED PROJECT

Here's everything we learned on gaining speed and hitting it farther.

THE ROAD TO 180

A normal 31-year-old dad trying to gain more speed.

From Cordie Walker

At the start of the year, I sat down to write my golf goals:

- Qualify for the State Am.
- Shoot under par in a tournament.

Then I stared at the page. Those were great goals, but they were also completely out of my control. I could train for months, show up on the first tee, and still have a bad day.

I needed a goal that was an actual indicator of progress. A metric that, if I hit it, would mean I was truly improving, putting in time to practice, not just hoping to peak at the right time.

That's when it hit me: 180 mph ball speed.

It's still an outcome goal, but it's something I can directly influence. Unlike "winning a tournament" or "qualifying for an event," it's a number that reflects the work I put in. If I do the right things – train properly, improve my swing, and get new equipment – my speed will go up.

So I broke it down further into process goals – the things I ***actually*** need to do to make 180 mph a reality:

- **Work out consistently:** Strength, mobility, and speed-specific training.
- **Speed training:** Spending time on the SKILL of speed.
- **Technique improvements:** Working with coaches to remove inefficiencies.
- **Club fitting:** Getting fit for clubs that max out my potential.

If I execute on these things week after week, there's ***no doubt*** this will help my entire game.

Where I'm Starting

Right now, my "gamer" ball speed is around ***165–170 mph***. On a really good swing, I can touch 175 mph. But to hit 180 mph consistently in tournament play, I need my clubhead speed to jump from 112–114 mph to at least 121–123 mph.

This is all about ***training speed as a skill.*** Too many golfers think they've maxed out their potential, but they haven't. They just haven't trained this skill.

In my book, it's a skill just like lag putting or distance control that you have to learn and practice.

I'm giving myself ***one year*** to make this happen.

I don't play golf for a living. I have a job, a family, and all the usual responsibilities. But I also know that if I want to get better, I have to train differently.

This is my journey to 180.

EPISODE 1: LUKE BENOIT

See the full video here!

I kicked things off with a speed lesson from Dr. Luke Benoit, the Rypstick creator and one of golf's most innovative coaches. We talked through speed training, and then he gave me a lesson on what I could do to pick up more speed.

"You don't just wake up one day swinging faster. You have to train it, and you have to push past what feels normal."

Concept #1: You're not training hard enough.

Let's be honest. You might think you're training for speed, but you're not. Most golfers go to the range and hit *comfortable* shots at *comfortable* speeds.

Real speed training is uncomfortable.

You need to ***train at the edge of chaos.*** If you don't feel out of control at times, you're not swinging hard enough.

The biggest mistake? *Not taking enough swings.* The research (and long-drive competitors) show that most golfers don't hit their fastest speeds until swing 30-40. If you're stopping after 10 balls, you're missing out.

Try this speed hack: The 40-Ball Speed Threshold

- Hit 10 balls "normally" at your game speed.
- Now, hit ***40 drivers at max effort,*** logging every 10 shots.
- What happened? By swing 30, ***you probably unlocked speeds you never hit before.***
- The lesson? ***You're stopping before your body actually adapts to moving faster.***

Concept #2: You're thinking about your backswing all wrong.

If you want more speed, you need a longer, looser backswing with three important changes:

1. **Flare your right elbow:** By allowing the right elbow to flare slightly at the top of the backswing, you create more external rotation, increasing the swing arc. This adjustment reduces power leaks and allows for greater clubhead speed, similar to what is seen in long drive competitors.
2. 
Extend the spine for more range: Maintaining a taller posture in the backswing increases the overall range of motion, enabling a deeper turn and more stored energy. This also allows for a smoother transition into the downswing without sacrificing control.
3. **Get more "across the line" without getting steep:** While an across-the-line backswing was traditionally discouraged, modern speed training suggests that a slight cross position can increase the length of the swing arc. However, it's important to maintain a shallow downswing to ensure optimal impact efficiency and prevent excessive spin.

Try this speed hack: The "Jack Nicklaus Drill"

- Take your normal backswing, but you should feel like you're intentionally over-exaggerating these three things. It should feel a little reckless at first.
- Now, check your launch monitor and see how much more clubhead speed you unlocked.

Here's one power leak Luke saw in my swing right away: "You're a little laid off at the top, and that's a power leak. You won't see long drive guys laid off – it's rare. More range equals more speed."

Concept #3: Your brain is slowing you down.

There's a reason you can't just *choose* to swing faster. ***Your brain is holding you back.*** Your nervous system has built-in "speed limiters" to protect you from losing balance or control.

"You have a governor on your speed. You think you're maxing out, but there's always more. You just need to push past what feels comfortable."

"If you don't train for speed, you won't have speed. It's that simple."

EPISODE 2-4: MARK BLACKBURN

I was excited to talk speed with Mark because I knew we'd go deep on the data from force plates and 3D motion capture – and boy, did we ever!

Force plates: What are they, and what do they measure?

Force plates are a platform with sensors that measure the forces you apply into the ground during your swing, known as Ground Reaction Forces (GRF). These plates tell us metrics like vertical force (upward push), horizontal force (side-to-side push), and torque (twisting force). When we look at all these forces we can figure out how effectively you're using the ground to create speed.

Here's the sequence we should be seeing those forces applied within the swing:

1. **Unweighting:** As you finish the backswing, your body should "float" as you reduce pressure under your feet by moving down faster than gravity. This unweights the system and sets up the chain reaction.
2. **Squat:** Immediately after unweighting, apply force into the ground. This mini-squat loads the system like a spring and stores energy for the jump.
3. **Jump:** Push vertically before impact. That upward force helps pull the handle up and back, decelerating your hands and releasing the clubhead like a whip.

Unweighting isn't lifting your lead foot in the backswing. It happens when your body drops faster than gravity in transition, creating a brief "float."

The more you unweight, the more you can push back up, like loading a spring. That upward force helps decelerate the handle and sling the clubhead faster.

What the Force Plates Revealed About My Swing

My analysis showed good news and bad news.

- **The good news:** I have great vertical force numbers! Mark said mine were even better than some tour players.
- **The bad news:** While my vertical force numbers were good, I wasn't using them effectively because my timing was off. Mark pointed out that instead of applying maximum vertical force as the club transitions from backswing to downswing, ***I was consistently too late.***

"The best players apply their vertical force early in transition – so by the time they're at lead-arm parallel, they're already peaking." Essentially, the forces I was generating never translated into real clubhead acceleration because my handle wasn't slowing down at the right moment.

"You're applying great force, but your timing's off. Your leg stays bent too long, preventing your handle from decelerating at the right time, so you never fully transfer that force into clubhead speed."

Mark demonstrated this idea using an Orange Whip training aid: "If you slow the handle down early enough, the head snaps forward quickly. If you're too late, you lose all that whip-like speed."

Kinematic Sequence: What 3D Data Told Us

Next, we looked at my kinematic sequence using 3D motion capture, which tracks how different parts of your body move through the swing.

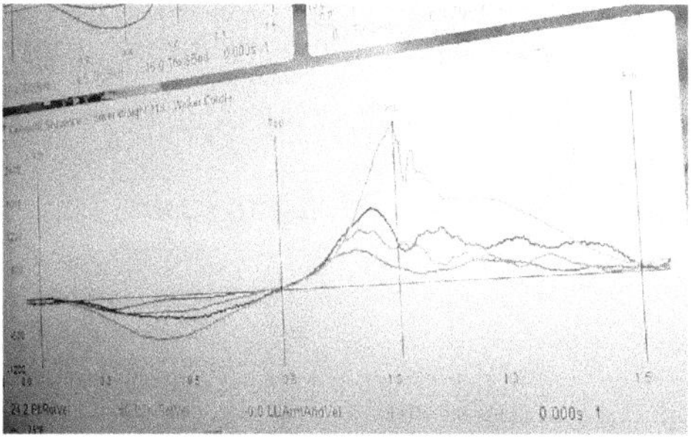

Ideally, the lower body initiates the downswing, followed by the torso, arms, and finally the clubhead. This creates a smooth chain reaction of acceleration and deceleration.

On the graphs, my pelvis generated strong initial force, but the torso's acceleration and deceleration patterns were fragmented and inconsistent.

Mark explained, "Your lower body creates energy exceptionally well, but your core isn't strong enough or coordinated enough to smoothly transfer that power to the arms and, ultimately, the club." This directly correlated to the late vertical force seen in my GRF data. The 3D system also pointed out that the weakest link might be coming from a ***core strength issue.***

My Core Weakness

To confirm this, Mark conducted a few quick physical tests:

- **Chest Pass (upper body power):** 21.5 ft. (good)
- **Vertical Jump (leg power):** 21 inches (good)
- **Sit-Up and Throw (core power):** 17–18 ft. (below average)

"Your core isn't just your abs – it's your glutes, hips, and trunk. It's the transmission system. Yours isn't effectively moving energy into the club. That's your primary leak."

Three Drills for Better Speed

Based on the data, Mark gave me three drills to help address these timing and strength issues:

1. **Half-Swing Jump Drill**

- Begin with your backswing, pausing when your lead arm is parallel to the ground.
- From this paused position, explosively jump upward while rotating through the swing.
- Focus on synchronizing the jump with your rotation to develop early vertical force and proper swing timing.

2. **Split-Grip Snap Drill**

- Grip your club with hands separated, similar to how you'd hold a hockey stick.
- Make short, aggressive swings, pulling the handle upward and inward quickly.
- This drill trains you to decelerate the handle effectively and feel the clubhead snap powerfully through impact.

3. **Med Ball Slam Drill**

- Take a golf stance holding an 8 lb. medicine ball.
- Take a backswing holding the ball.
- Slam the ball into the ground, and feel the force going into the ball of the lead foot.

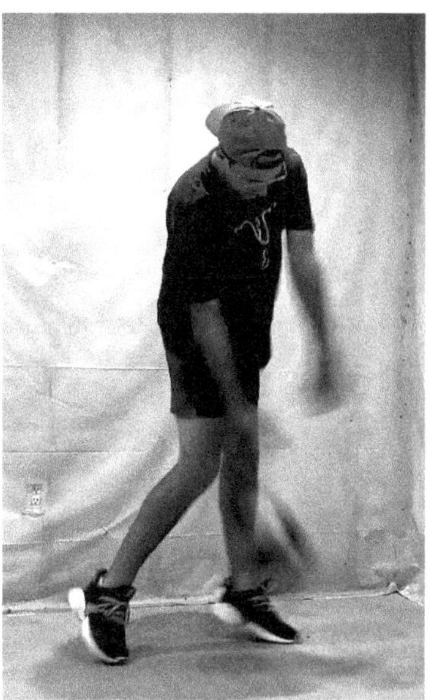
Med Ball Slam Drill

What This Means Going Forward

"You've got the engine, but your transmission is lacking. We need to build a stronger, better-coordinated core."

Ultimately, the path to more speed involves:

- Improving core strength.
- Practicing drills to improve my timing of vertical forces.

"***Speed isn't magic. It's a learned skill.*** Train it deliberately, measure your progress, and you'll see ***dramatic breakthroughs.***"

DIY Fitness Test for Speed

Want to know if your body is holding you back from gaining speed? Do these three tests at home or the gym with a 8 lb. medicine ball and tape measure.

1. **Chest Pass**

- Sit and throw a med ball from your chest as far as you can. This measures upper body strength.
- *Benchmark:* 21–22 feet is average for tour-level speed potential.

2. Sit-Up & Throw

- Lie on your back with the ball above your head. Do a sit-up and throw the ball forward. This measures core strength.
- *Benchmark:* Within 2–3 feet of your chest pass. If not, you have a core power leak.

3. Vertical Jump

- Stand and jump as high as possible. This measures lower body explosiveness.
- *Benchmark:* 20+ inches is solid for golfers looking to hit 180+ mph ball speed.

My Results from Testing with Mark:

- Chest Pass: about 21.5 ft. – success!
- Sit-Up & Throw: about 17–18 ft. – fail (3–4.5 ft. behind chest pass)
- Vertical Jump: 21 inches – success!

"You've got great ground reaction forces, but you're not putting them in the club. The missing link is your core's ability to transfer that energy.

The core isn't just your stomach; it's your glutes, hips, and trunk, too. It's the transmission. We just need to build a stronger one." – Mark Blackburn

EPISODE 5: NICK CLEARWATER & MARK CROSSFIELD

See the full video here!

Toward the middle of summer, I was at a video shoot with ***Mark Crossfield*** and ***Nick Clearwater*** and had the opportunity to get their feedback on my road to 180.

Mark had gained a bunch of speed over the last couple of years, so I wanted to hear his biggest takeaways – and it's similar to what I've learned: get the body in shape to be able to deal with the forces needed for more speed, have the intention to hit it hard, and don't be afraid about contact and focus on swinging faster.

> "Every time you go to the bathroom, do some kind of exercise like push-ups, squats, etc. Bring fitness into your day-to-day if it's hard for you to set aside time for working out."
> – Mark Crossfield

We chatted through what I had worked on with Mark Blackburn, and Nick had a great drill for me to understand how to move the body to improve the timing of the vertical force.

The Half-Swing Drill

"By the time your shaft reaches parallel on the downswing, you need to stop bending forward and start extending upward. This short drill forces you to condense that entire movement into a split second, making it easier to feel and execute."

Here's what to do:

1. Only take the club back until your lead arm is parallel to the ground. Keep it compact.
2. From this position, fire your legs, hips, chest, and arms upward and backward – like someone launching off a ski jump.
3. Stop your swing shortly after impact, fully extended and tall.

"This move teaches your body how to spike ground reaction forces in an instant. It trains your motor program to generate speed efficiently and explosively."

Real Results...and a Bit of Chaos

The first few swings were wild – I even skied one. Nick actually knew why: "When you pop one up, it shows you're still bent too far forward at impact. Keep working until you naturally start extending upward sooner."

"Most golfers misunderstand vertical extension. The half-swing drill simplifies it. Even if you never hit the ball past your normal distance during practice, you'll suddenly find new, untapped speed in your full swing."

EPISODE 6-7: JON SINCLAIR

See the full video here!

Over the course of the summer, I gained speed, but my distance was stuck – so I traveled to Dallas to work with Jon Sinclair, one of golf's leading club fitters and coaches, to get dialed into the perfect driver head and shaft combination to maximize distance.

My Original Driver

I'd been gaming the same driver for nearly five years. I loved it and trusted it, but my swing speed had only jumped from around 113 mph to 117 mph on the golf course.

- My spin numbers hovered around 3500 RPM.
- I consistently missed just low on the clubface.

Shaft Secrets: Understanding Torque vs. Flex

Here's something I never fully grasped until this fitting: Torque is just as crucial as shaft flex.

- ***Torque*** measures how much a shaft twists during your swing.
- ***Flex*** measures how much it bends.

"Most golfers obsess over flex and ignore torque, but torque dramatically impacts feel, accuracy, and distance."

For example, when we tested a shaft with slightly lower torque (the TPT 16 Lo), my ball flight immediately tightened up, accuracy improved dramatically, and it became significantly easier to square the clubface.

With the TPT shafts, because the torque was lower, I could comfortably swing a shaft with more flex without losing control.

When we dialed in the correct loft and shaft combo, the results were ***awesome***:

- ***My ball speed jumped to 177 mph,*** which was previously unthinkable!
- ***My carry distance stretched consistently beyond 310 yards,*** hitting a peak of 318 yards during our fitting.

Jon's take on club fitting is simple and effective: "Your club fitting should never force you to adapt to the club. It should match your natural swing so closely that you instantly perform better."

My Lesson with Jon

After our driver fitting, I asked Jon to dive into some data and see if I'd made progress with my vertical forces and to get his take on my speed journey.

Well.

My vertical forces were still too late, so Jon had a few concepts to help with a deeper understanding of that.

Concept #1: Moment Arm

The moment arm is how far your center of pressure moves away from your center of mass – basically, it's torque. The more separation you get between the pressure and your body's mass, the more potential to generate force.

My issue? My center of pressure wasn't moving far enough, early enough. I was pushing up too late, not creating enough torque to whip the club.

Concept #2: Understanding Hand Speed (And Why It Needs to Slow Down)

Jon introduced another new concept: hand speed.

- Hand speed isn't just about going fast; it's about the timing.
- Ideally, your hands should reach their ***maximum speed before impact*** and then start slowing down.
- That deceleration acts like a whip, transferring energy to the clubhead.
- "Faster hands aren't the goal. Better timing is."

In our session:

- My hands were initially peaking at around 21 mph but weren't slowing down in time.
- Once I started pushing earlier and more efficiently, my hand speed jumped to 27 mph, then decelerated at just the right moment. That's when the club starts doing the work.

Concept #3: The Band Pull Stability Check

I love it when a drill helps you feel what ***should*** be happening, and this was a really unique way to feel how the forces should be applied!

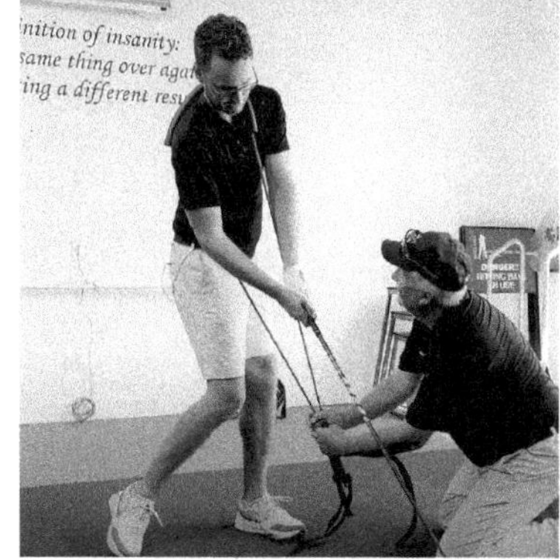

- Set up to the ball in your normal address position.
- Have someone stand in front and pull your club forward and slightly down with their hands or a resistance band.
- Notice if you feel stable or unstable.

What I felt: Weak and unstable when pressure came from the front. I wasn't counterbalancing the swing properly.

Why it matters: You can't accelerate fast if you're unstable. This drill teaches your body what it feels like to resist the force of a fast-moving club at the right place.

Concept #4: Slider Lead Foot Drill

To help me feel the proper ground push, Jon had me put my lead foot on a slider.

- During the downswing, push back against the ground using your lead leg at about a 45-degree angle.
- Let the slider help you feel the motion of pushing ***back and away*** from the target.

This gets you pushing in the right direction at the right time. That backward push helps your hands release and slow down, like cracking a whip.

Here's what the data showed:

- Hand speed jumped from 21 mph to 27 mph after changing the timing of my push.
- Vertical force peaked earlier – closer to lead-arm parallel rather than at impact.
- That led to better deceleration of my hands, which helps transfer energy into the club.

"When you release correctly, speed gets easier – not harder."

EPISODE 8: KOLBY TULLIER'S SECRET TO BOOSTING SWING SPEED IN THE GYM

 the-stable.com

 kolbywayne

 See the full video here!

"You're never going to be able to do it if you can't get the hip to turn." That was the moment I realized I'd been skipping a crucial piece of the Road to 180: my body.

After months of chasing speed on the range, I finally stepped into one of golf's top performance gyms, to work with Kolby Tullier, the guy who helps tour players get faster and stay healthy.

And let's just say, it got humbling fast.

Part One: The Assessment

Before we started any training, Kolby wanted to see how my body moved.

"We're trying to apply force into the golf club to transfer it into the golf ball. ***If the body can't move the right way, that force never transfers."***

He began with a hip mobility test (see right):

- **Right hip internal rotation:** 23°
- **Left hip internal rotation:** 30°
- **Tour average:** 50°+

"My top golfers have over 50," he said. "That's what lets them stay in posture and really load the trail side." And if you struggle with that... "Either you're going to over-rotate the thoracic spine, or you're going to lift the club up with your arms and hands."

Then came the glute tests. When I lifted into a bridge, I felt it in my hamstrings instead of my glutes. "If you feel it in your hamstrings, your glutes are shut off," Kolby said. "If the glutes don't work, the hips aren't mobile. And if the hips aren't mobile, your swing is fighting itself."

Finally, we moved to three Oxefit power tests: vertical jump, rotary power, and anti-rotation. They measured how much force I could create and how evenly I used both sides of my body.

- **Vertical jump:** 17 inches
- **Peak force:** 336 lbs
- **Load balance:** 28% more on my right side
- **Rotational strength:** stronger turning left than right

Kolby said every player has something like this. His job is to find the weak links before adding speed work. For me, the pattern was clear: limited hip mobility, inactive glutes, and an uneven lower body. All of it tied together.

Part Two: The Fix

Once Kolby identified the weak links, we started rebuilding from the ground up. He had me working on golf-specific movements that taught me to push, rotate, and stabilize while using my whole body. Below are a couple of examples. Check out ***all*** of them here:

Drills we did:

1. Core Circles

Start in a push-up position with one leg lifted slightly off the ground. Move that leg in slow, controlled circles to open up the hips and wake up the core. The goal is to stay steady through the upper body while the hips move freely.

2. Cable Hip Rotations

Use a cable machine or resistance band set at waist height. Stand perpendicular to the cable with the handle near your chest, trail foot grounded through the inside edge and big toe. Push into the ground and rotate your hips against the resistance. You'll quickly learn whether you can stay stable and rotate through the trail hip or if your body wants to tip, slide, or lift.

3. Speed Rotations

Attach a light resistance band at chest height. Make fast, explosive rotations back and through while keeping your lower body grounded. These short bursts train your body and brain to move faster without losing your balance.

4. Contrast Training

Do four heavy goblet squats, then immediately follow with four box jumps. The squats build force, and the jumps teach you to use that force quickly. This pairing develops the ability to produce power on demand – the same skill that drives clubhead speed.

> "Everything we do has to transfer to the swing. I'm not chasing numbers on a leg press. I'm training movement." – Kolby Tullier

What stood out was how clearly the gym work matched what happens in the swing. Kolby even pointed out that my weight tends to move toward my toes – something I've seen confirmed on force plates. The gym and swing data lined up perfectly.

What I learned from Kolby is simple: if I want more speed, I need a stronger, more stable body. But the way he trains it is different. It's not generic strength work; it's movement built for golfers.

KOLBY'S TRAINING TRUTHS

Kolby trains some of the fastest players in golf, but his approach isn't about lifting more weight; it's about ***moving better.*** Here are a few of his go-to principles.

1. Don't build a cannon on a canoe.

You can't stack power on an unstable foundation. If your base (e.g. your hips, glutes, and core) is weak, adding strength just builds bad patterns. Build stability first, ***then*** add power.

2. Build strength that transfers.

Kolby's creating exercises that have three core components: pushing, rotating, and stabilizing. ***Everything*** connects back to how the body moves through a swing.

3. Train fast to move fast.

Most golfers get stronger slowly and never move fast. "Strength is one thing. Speed is another. You have to train the brain to ***move faster***," says Kolby.

4. Fix the imbalances first.

Every athlete has a stronger, more stable side. Kolby finds and corrects those gaps before adding speed work. Everyone wants speed ***right now***, but if you don't fix the imbalances, it won't transfer.

5. Recovery is part of the program.

Cold plunges, saunas, sleep, and nutrition all matter. Recovery is just as important as training. The body can't adapt if it's exhausted.

WANT MY BEST SPEED HACKS?!

Here's a summary of all the hacks that have worked for me in my testing! Try them out, and see what works best for you.

Treat the warm-up like a workout.

Most golfers think a warm-up is touching your toes and doing some air swings with a 7-iron. What really helped me? A full-on gym session before I hit balls.

20–30 minutes in the gym. Heavy lifts. Explosive movements.

The goal: ***Wake up the big muscles. Load. Turn. Explode.***

The biggest difference-makers:

- Resistance band loading drills
- Medicine ball throws
- Quick hip/glute mobility
- And this big one: ***Move fast in the gym so you can move fast in your swing.*** Not everything should be slow and controlled.

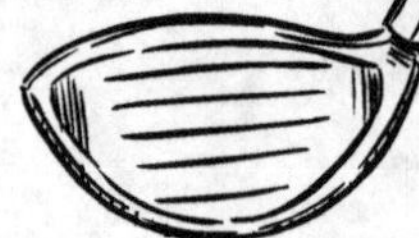

Setup tweaks that actually matter:

- **Flaring both feet** – especially the lead foot – helps you rotate. Go extreme here. 45° feels weird, but ***weird = good.***
- **Grip pressure** – stronger than you think. Long drive guys and tour pros don't hold it like a baby bird.
- **Wider stance** – just look at guys who mash it. Feels awkward. Works wonders.

The backswing is your speed multiplier.

This was a game-changer. Length and speed in the backswing ***directly impact*** how much force you can create.

- **Go Jon Daly-long.** Hands way up. Trail elbow flared. Reach for the sky.
- **Rip it back fast.** Like, aggressively fast. The combo of long + fast = more force.
- **Lose sight of the ball.** Seriously. You're moving off it more, pressure into the trail side, and lifting that lead foot? That's a *good* sign.
- Feels to try:
    - Trail hip rising like you're standing up
    - Pressure shift way back – like you're almost swaying
- **Lead foot lift = better rotation + a trigger for the downswing**

VIDEO FOR REAL-TIME FEEDBACK:

Here's the thing: when you "try something," you're probably not doing it anywhere near enough. That's why ***instant video feedback is non-negotiable.*** You have to ***overdo it to actually do it.*** If it doesn't feel crazy, you're not changing.

Pre-swing triggers: stay loose and move fast.

Ever notice Kyle Berkshire's little bounce before he launches one into orbit?

- ***Rocking pressure side-to-side before the swing*** keeps your body primed and fast.
- It's a trigger. It's a rhythm thing. And it works. Try it before your next speed session. Feel the bounce, then launch.

The weirdest (but best) concept: up-down-up.

This one is wild. Imagine your swing like a chop:

1. **Up** in the backswing.
2. **Down** to load.
3. **Up** again to explode through.

That vertical movement feels awkward at first, but it leads to ***huge speed gains*** because you're applying vertical force at the right time.

Downswing keys that made the difference:

This is where I left the most speed on the table – and worked the hardest to change.

- **Don't hold the lag too long.** Your hands should be flying when your lead arm is *parallel* on the way down. You're not saving speed for impact – you're releasing it early, so it whips.
- **Peak vertical force should happen early.** Ideally, when that lead arm hits parallel. If you wait till impact, you've missed it. You're pushing so hard into the ground off the ball of your lead foot, it's pushing you back.
- **The feel you're looking for is "jump early."**

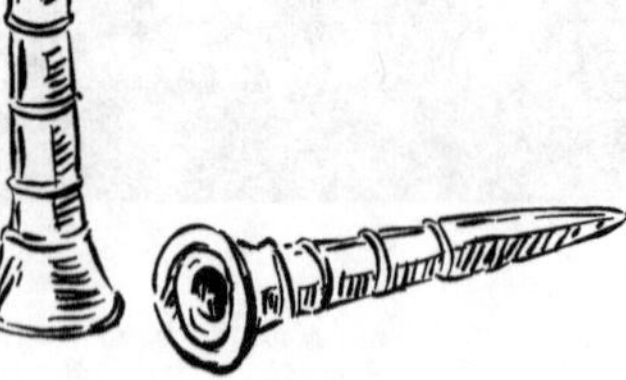

WRAPPING UP THE ROAD TO 180 IN 2024

When I started this project, I wasn't sure if 180 was even possible. I knew I needed to swing faster. I knew I needed to train harder. But I didn't know what it would actually take to get there.

Over the year, I kept chipping away. Speed training at home. Trying *(keyword: trying)* to get in the gym consistently. There were weeks where things went great, and it all came together, and then a 2-3 week stretch where I wouldn't work out or speed train.

Despite my inconsistency, by September, ***I hit a 181 mph ball speed.*** And by December, I reached 182.

That's an 8 mph gain from where I started the year – ***174 to 182.***

But here's the part that really got me excited.

I wasn't just peaking at 180+ once every 20 swings. I could cruise in the high 170s, even when I wasn't swinging out of my shoes. The effort level to reach 175–177 went way down.

What's next? The Road to 190.

We're not done.

Next year, the journey continues with a new goal: ***190 mph ball speed.*** It's going to take a lot more consistent work, but I'm ready to double down and make it happen.

Speed is a skill – something you can train and grow.

On the Road to 190. Let's go.

GOLFWELL · GOLFWELL · GOLFWELL

BEST OF GOLFWELL

Weekly

Don't miss a single newsletter every Thursday morning!

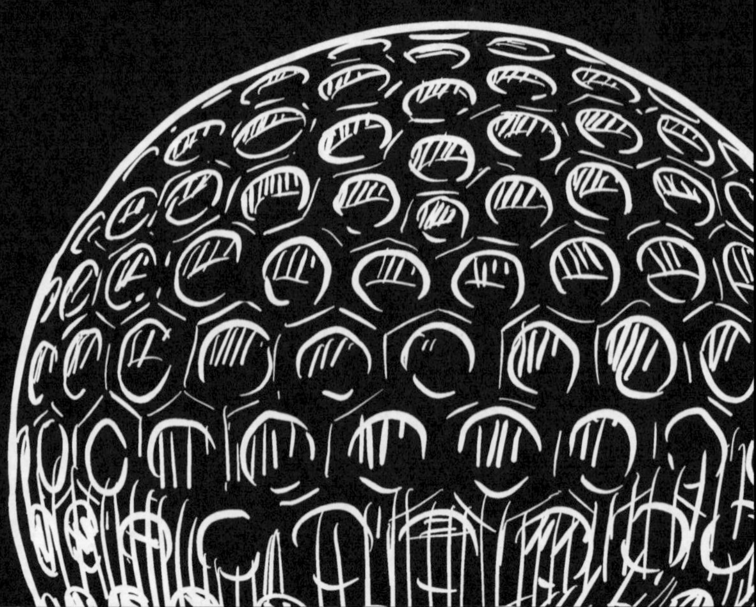

HOW DO I SHAVE SEVEN SHOTS OFF MY SCORE IN SEVEN MINUTES?

It was a sarcastic question, but I have a serious reply.

1. The more you can hit putter around the green instead of a lob wedge, you'll hit it closer and give yourself a better chance to get up and down.

Shotscope data says that scratch players are almost ***twice*** as likely to get up and down with a putter compared to live wedge, and 25 handicappers are almost ***six*** times more likely.

2. Chill out on lag putts.

PGA tour pros are more likely to three-putt than make a putt outside of 33 feet, so just hit it close and do your best to two-putt. Grind on the speed, not on the line.

3. Don't skip your warm-up!

A 2022 study found that golfers who didn't perform an appropriate warm-up prior to teeing off were 3.2 times more likely to get injured.

Seriously. Get your body in a state that's ready to move and function at speed.

4. Understand dispersion patterns and do some testing (with your driver and irons).

A rule of thumb is "10% miss right and left for the yardage" – in other words, a 150-yard shot 15 yards left and right. But test it out! Hit 10–20 shots on a simulator and see what yours actually is. Stop aiming at pins and see the range of areas your shots could go into.

5. Find the largest part of the green and aim there. Avoid shortsiding yourself at all costs, as that's a guaranteed way to increase your scoring average.

One of your goals for any approach strategy should be to avoid shortsiding yourself.

6. Mindset reframe: Bogeys are okay.

Chip it on the green, get your two-putt, and go to the next hole. Whatever you do, ***don't make double bogeys.*** Play the safer shot that has a higher probability of success, even if it means you're likely to just make a bogey.

7. Set better goals and get your focus off score.

Instead of setting vague or unrealistic goals like "I want to break 80," set specific and measurable targets that you can track and work towards. For me, making golf fun and getting more practice involved picking a speed goal, so I spent more time in the gym and training. Maybe it's a new goal and pursuit that gets you motivated and working on your game!

SEVEN OUT-OF-THE-BOX IDEAS TO BRING YOU BACK TO THE PRESENT

Your best performance happens when you're fully present and in the moment, not dwelling on the past shot or future hole you're freaked out by. But how the heck do you stay present? Focus on your breath? Talk with your playing partners? Stop talking to your playing partners?

Here are a few ideas that you might not have heard of that could help that I learned from Dr. Greg Cartin. They embrace the concept of "novel distinction."

1. Use an object to bring you back to the present.

Carry a small object like a coin or stone in your pocket, or jot down a motivational quote on your glove. Whenever you feel your focus waning, touch, or look at it to ground yourself in the present.

2. One-sense focus.

Dedicate a hole or a few shots to honing in on just one of your senses. Feel the turf under your shoes, listen to the rustle of leaves, or watch the clouds drift by to anchor yourself in the moment.

3. Watch your next shot in reverse.

Start with where the ball finishes and watch it all the way back to your present moment. This can provide a totally new perspective on where you are and challenge you to think creatively about the next shot.

4. Practice gratitude to get your head in the right state before playing.

Before a round, take a moment to write down three things you are grateful for. Go back to that list throughout the round to change your thought process if you get distracted from the present.

5. Mindful snacking (before you ignore this one, just try it).

Practice mindful eating during your round. Take time to savor and enjoy any food you eat during a round, paying attention to the taste, texture, and smell of the food.

6. Try using your non-dominant hand for teeing the ball up or marking your ball on the green.

This act of "novel distinction" can help bring your attention to the present moment and also challenge you to develop new skills.

Don't try all of these strategies at once. If you struggle to stay present or get nervous easily, and you're looking for ways to not let your mind run wild, try one of these tests one at a time. Figure out what works for you.

WHAT'S YOUR BEST AND WORST ROUND OF THE YEAR?!

Here's the deal. Set good expectations. Every time you show up to the golf course, you could shoot anywhere in a wide range of scores.

I asked folks on X (you may also know it as Twitter) to share their best and worst scores of the year, and the results are pretty interesting. For me and my season, it was a low of 70 and a high of 85. That's a ***BIG*** difference, but I was below the average with my spread of scores!

Remember this before you tee it up next time.

Cordie Walker | GolfWell @cordie_golfwell · Sep 9 Promote ···

What's the difference between your best round of the year and worst?

34 4 16K

Cordie Walker | GolfWell @cordie_golfwell · Sep 11 ···

As of right now 24 of you replied with scores. Here how that shakes out!

I always forget just how big of a range scores can be through a season.

Hopefully this is a good reminder that even though you have one bad day it doesn't define your season.

Low	High	Difference	
74.4	91.5	17.0	Average
74.5	90	16.5	Median

3 818

FOUR REMINDERS FOR YOUR NEXT PRACTICE SESSION

1. THE BIG MYTH is that making errors in practice is going to promote making more errors in performance.

An effective learning environment is going to challenge the learner, and a byproduct of that is mistakes. Mistakes and failure are part of the learning process!

2. Focus on long-term learning, not short-term performance.

Don't worry too much about how well you perform during practice. Instead, focus on challenging yourself to optimize long-term learning.

3. With too *much* or too *little* difficulty during your practice, your learning is minimized.

The goal is to be optimally challenged for success ***during*** the round, not success during practice.

4. Seek the sweet spot of challenge.

Aim for a 65–70% success rate in your practice. It's okay to fail about 30–35% of the time, as it helps in long-term learning.

TWO MENTAL STRATEGIES FOR YOUR NEXT COMPETITIVE ROUND

"I knew my mind would wander. I'd get caught up in score or pissed off about a bad shot." These are thoughts we ***all*** have, from tour pro to 20 handicap. So when preparing for some tournaments this past week, I leaned on two mindfulness tactics.

And I'll be honest, these ***really, really*** helped me. They gave me something to do when I started to get lost in the emotions of score or a bad shot, and I think these can help you as well.

The 5-4-3-2-1 Grounding Exercise

The 5-4-3-2-1 is a great task-based grounding exercise that gives you something to do between shots or while you have a long wait:

- ***5 Colors:*** Look around and find five different colors. Notice the shades and tones, like the different colors of green in the fairway or the trees in the distance.
- ***4 Sounds:*** Close your eyes and listen for four distinct sounds. It could be the wind, birds, or clubs rattling in your golf bag.
- ***3 Textures:*** Focus on three textures you can feel. This might be your golf glove, shoes on your feet, or the shirt you're wearing on your arms.

- ***2 Scents:*** Take a deep breath and identify two smells. Maybe it's the fresh-cut grass or your sunscreen. (I struggled with this one!)
- ***1 Deep Breath:*** Finally, take one deep breath to center yourself.

This technique helps shift your focus from anxious thoughts to the present moment by engaging your senses, thus grounding you in reality.

Here's the part that really helps us as emotional, often anxious, golfers: studies suggest that it promotes sensory awareness, interrupts the anxiety loop, and activates neural pathways associated with awareness and attention.

The Box Breathing Technique

Controlled breathing can help calm your mind and body. Box breathing is simple:

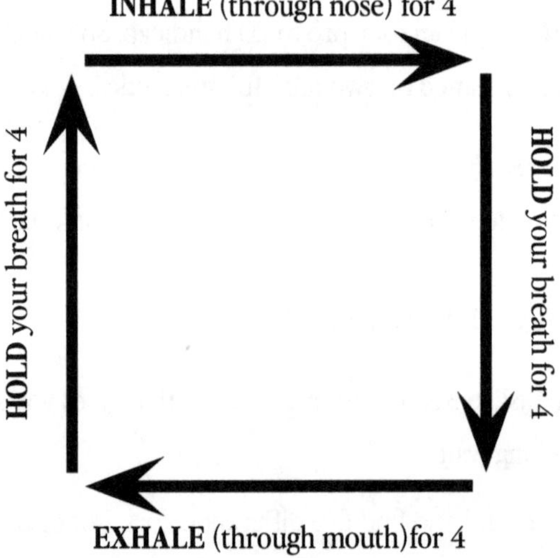

Repeat this cycle 4–5 times. This helps regulate your breathing and keeps you calm.

JUST FIVE MINUTES

You want to improve. You want to get better. But you find it hard to actually do the things that you know will help you get there.

We have a goal. We know the actions to get us there. But how do we actually ***do*** those things when we're tired and stressed, and life is busy?

Maybe just do five minutes.

Go through your putting routine and practice for ***just five minutes.***

Do some speed training for ***just five minutes.***

Go for a run for ***just five minutes.***

And what you might find is that you ***can*** commit to just five minutes. That's not hard. Anyone can do that.

But you might find that after five minutes, you might as well keep going – you're already there, and you might as well.

So next time you find yourself reluctant to tackle that next action to get you towards your goal, just try it for five minutes, and see what happens.

FIELD EXPERIMENT: THE TRIPLE THREAT CHALLENGE

Location: Practice Green **Skill:** Short Game **Skill Level:** Intermediate

How to Play

- Grab three golf balls and your go-to wedge for around the green.
- Find nine unique shots around the green. Start with shots that are 3–6 yards off the green.
- Drop three balls at each spot.
- With each shot, hit a different type of shot: one low, one medium, and one high.

Scoring

Track score for each type of shot.

- Within four feet = 3 points
- Within 15 feet = 1 point
- Didn't execute the shot loft = -1 point

Review

- What shot had the best score?
- What type of shot did you find most comfortable?
- Did one shot shape surprise you?
- Did you stay mentally engaged and interested in the game?

FIELD EXPERIMENT: FOUR AWARENESS DRILLS TO GET UNSTUCK

Experiment 1: Tempo

On the range, hit shots at 20%, 50%, 80%, 100%, and 110%. (20% and 110% are the crucial ones!) Really try to hit it slow and see if you can only hit a 7-iron 50 yards or less with 20% tempo. It's a unique experience!

- What do you learn?
- How does your backswing feel?
- What do you notice about your quality of strike at a slower speed?

Experiment 2: Shot Shape

No matter what your stock shot is, try to hit the biggest slice you can and biggest hook you can with a 3-wood, then a 5-iron, then a 7-iron.

- Is one easier than another for you?
- How long does it take you to accomplish each type of shot?

Experiment 3: Setup

Hit shots with a 6-iron with these different setups:

- Ball position middle of stance. Ball position off front foot. Ball position off back foot.
- Ball farther away so arms are extended. Ball closer than normal to body. Ball in normal position.
- Hit a shot where you line your feet up 20 yards left of the target, then try to hit it at the flag. Do the same to the right of the target. Then line up straight at the target.

Experiment 4: Swing Shape

Take the club back normally, take it more outside, and then take it back inside. After that, take a normal backswing and try to move your path to the right, normal, and to the left.

How does each feel, and what happens to the ball flight?

These drills build create more awareness of your swing and body. Awareness is a superpower on the course. No need for panic buttons. Just a calm, mindful observation, and you're back on track.

Use these drills to help you gain awareness and get unstuck!

CORDIE'S THREE KEYS TO SPEED

As a junior golfer, you wouldn't say that my driver was my go-to club. I remember always fighting snap hooks and having such a hard time keeping the ball in play.

There was a starting hole at our school's home course with OB left, and I still have scar tissue from standing on the tee box thinking about hooking shots into those woods.

Nothing better than hooking a ball into the woods and starting with a triple on hole #1 as a freshman in high school, trying to be cool and stay on the varsity team.

However, strokes gained off the tee have turned into my number one strength. I reflected back on what changed and found these three keys I want to go through today.

Key 1: Find the Right Shaft Profile

At a PGA show, probably around 5-6 years ago, I got a quick shaft fitting from Jon Sinclair into a TPT shaft and a Ping G400 with some more flex than I was used to (I found an old video showing this; scan the QR code here). ⟶

It was great getting a new driver, but I didn't think much of it that spring. That summer, I started tracking strokes gained stats with Mark Broadie's app and learned that driver had become the ***strongest part of my game...by a lot.***

With the right setup, I suddenly found a weapon that launched the ball at the right launch angle and felt great to swing. The odd thing was I went to a shaft that had what felt like ***a lot of flex.*** It had a low kick point so you could really feel it bend towards the driver head, and that low kick felt good in my swing and got the ball launched higher for me with not too much spin.

My question for you is: Have you tried a shaft with ***more flex*** than you're used to lately?

The lesson here is that sticking with the conventional, "I have XXX mph swing speed, so I must play this shaft," is probably hurting you.

One crazy fact I learned along the way is that most long drive pros are using a regular, or in some cases, senior flex shaft. I couldn't believe they would use so much flex and work to time it up to optimize launch and speed.

Now it's not the most accurate or stable combo, but there is a lesson there.

If you've historically fought your driver, I can't recommend enough getting a fitting and trying shafts with different kick points and flex to really see what works best for you.

Key 2: Figure Out Where to Aim and Why

This new driver helped, but I was still a pretty conservative player. I would default to pulling back to a 4-iron or hybrid and keep the driver in the bag, even if I was hitting it well.

I didn't understand dispersion patterns or how to aim.

A breakthrough moment was talking with Scott Fawcett and learning how every tour player, on average, hits their driver with about a 65–70 yard dispersion. So you just need to find a 65–70 yard wide spot on each hole, and if there's not OB or water, blast away at the center target of where you can aim your dispersion pattern. ***GAME CHANGER.***

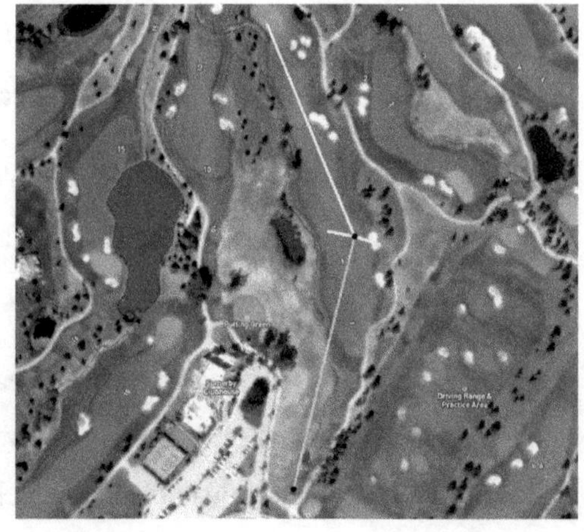

This concept gives you freedom to swing freely with the driver and know that you won't lose a ball.

Now, if I'm playing a new course, I'll pull up his Decade app or go through Google Maps before the round and figure out exactly where to aim so I won't lose a ball, and suddenly a lot of stress and tension fades away with this plan in place.

What most people don't realize is when you're hitting the driver, you have to get rid of the notion that you're aiming a sniper rifle and hitting it right on your spot.

You actually have a shotgun and need to center that blast in the area that gives you the highest chance of keeping the ball in play and going as far down the hole as possible.

And in my opinion, you have to map this out while looking at GPS or, well, a map. It's just too deceiving to try and figure out the 70-yard wide landing spot unless you're getting the facts from a map.

What you might realize is that there's tons of room in the rough or not on the fairway, so you'll need to start aiming away from the center of the fairway – but the increased distance (even though it's in the rough) will benefit you when looking at the strokes gained data.

The results of playing with clear targets will be hitting more drivers and keeping the ball in play more consistently. Hit it as far as you can, and don't lose golf balls!

Key 3: Actually Try to Hit It Farther

Some simple data that makes this clear is Shotscope, looking at the scores of a 5-handicap. When making birdie or better, average driving distance was 270; par or better, 258 yards; bogey or worse, 247 yards. Simply put, the lower scores came from the farther drives.

It reminds me of my junior golf days – how so many teachers and coaches commented about guys "swinging too hard" and how you should try and swing slower. I know I heard that about my swing, and I really believed that I was swinging too fast.

	5-Handicap	15-Handicap	25-Handicap
When making birdie or better	270 yards	257 yards	212 yards
When making par or better	258 yards	244 yards	193 yards
When making bogey or worse	247 yards	231 yards	184 yards

Now, I think the language of those conversations really screwed up a lot of people. I don't think it was an issue of swinging too fast. I think they were pinpointing another issue like swing sequencing and strength issues. So over the years, I've worked on gaining speed – in fact, we have a whole section of this book on it!

I've hung out with long-drive guys like Seb Twaddell and gotten myself accustomed to what more speed looks like and the potential I have. I've hit 124mph in training sessions with my driver, so I know I have more speed to unlock. For me, I know it comes down to getting stronger. This is the key to consistently improving my gaming speed up.

My prediction is that we see speed training become another skill that fundamental golfers practice just as regularly as something like chipping or putting. Most people just have never tried to "swing hard" and have done absolutely nothing to gain speed. They've talked about how much hitting it farther would help, but it takes ***training and practice.***

So the simple keys that have actually impacted my game?

1. Train it because it's a skill to learn.
2. Choose better targets so you're making confident swings to proper targets.
3. Don't settle for just an "okay" driver and shaft combo.

WRAPPING UP

Thanks for spending time with this guide, and a big thank you to every coach, player, and expert who shared their insights. This book exists because of them, and because you're willing to put the ideas into practice.

Golfwell is about helping golfers improve with research, great coaching, and smarter practice. If something in these pages helped you think differently, I hope you stick around for what's coming next.

The plan is to release a new version of this guide every year with the latest lessons from the smartest people in golf.

If you want to stay up to date, the best place is the YouTube channel and the weekly newsletter (scan the QR codes below to get there now)! New videos drop all the time, and the newsletter is where I share the most interesting ideas, drills, tools, and research I find each week.

See you out there.

FOLLOW GOLFWELL

YouTube
@golfwelltv

Newsletter: Golfwell Weekly

www.ingramcontent.com/pod-product-compliance
Lightning Source LLC
LaVergne TN
LVHW081325110826
845149LV00007B/1593

* 9 7 9 8 9 9 4 4 9 1 0 0 3 *